D1242132

Schiller's Aesthetic Essays

Schiller's Aesthetic Essays
Two Centuries of Criticism

Lesley Sharpe

Schiller's Aesthetic Essays:

Two Centuries of Criticism

CAMDEN HOUSE

Copyright © 1995 by
CAMDEN HOUSE, INC.

Published by Camden House, Inc.
Drawer 2025
Columbia, SC 29202 USA

Printed on acid-free paper.
Binding materials are chosen for strength and
durability.

ISBN 1–57113–058–6

Library of Congress Cataloging-in-Publication Data

Sharpe, Lesley.
    Schiller's aesthetic essays : two centuries of criticism / Lesley Sharpe.
    p.   cm.   -- (Studies in German literature, linguistics, and culture)
    Includes bibliographical references and index.
    ISBN 1-57113-058-6 (alk. paper)
    1. Schiller, Friedrich, 1759-1805--Aesthetics. 2. Schiller, Friedrich, 1759-
1805. Über die ästhetische Erziehung des Menschen. I. Title.
II. Series Studies in German literature, linguistics, and culture (Unnumbered)
PT2496.E8S5   1995
831'.6--dc20   95-292
                                                                CIP

Acknowledgments

I should like to take the opportunity to thank the Alexander von Humboldt-Stiftung for generously allowing me to resume my Research Fellowship and thus making possible an extended stay in Germany, where I gathered material at the Deutsches Literaturarchiv in Marbach. I am most grateful to the library staff there for their help and friendliness. My Department at the University of Exeter generously allowed me a year's leave of absence. I have profited from the advice and encouragement of my colleagues David Pugh and Edgar Yates, from the helpful comments of Norbert Oellers, the series editors James Hardin and Eitel Timm, and from the careful work of my copy-editor, Phil Dematteis. The shortcomings of this study are entirely my own responsibility.

LS

Contents

Preface   xi

Introduction: The Aesthetic Essays in Outline   1

1. The First Half-Century   7

2. Schiller's Aesthetics Discovered   20
    The First Wave   20
    The Empirical Approach   24
    Philosophical Approaches   26
    The Germanists   28
    The 1905 Centenary   31
    Schiller's Aesthetics outside the German-speaking World   35

3. From 1905 to 1945   39
    General Studies and the Impact of Geistesgeschichte   40
    Detailed Studies   45
    Schiller's Aesthetics Abroad   51

4. The Postwar Boom   58
    Editions and General Studies   59
    The Beautiful   67
    The Sublime   70
    Schiller, Kant and Other Philosophers   75
    Marxist Approaches   86
    The Aesthetic State: Social and Political Implications   94
    The Enlightenment Tradition and Anthropology   101
    The Rhetorical Tradition   103
    Über naive und sentimentalische Dichtung   108

Postscript   116

Works Consulted   117
    Schiller's principal writings on aesthetics   117
    Selected editions and translations   118
    Secondary literature   119

Index   133

Preface

THE CRITICISM OF Friedrich Schiller's aesthetics presents the reader with views of the hidden Schiller. The familiar playwright, whose quotable lines quickly became proverbs, whose poems were learned by heart by generations of German schoolchildren, and whose "Ode to Joy," a fervent affirmation of universal brotherhood, was set to music by Beethoven in his Ninth Symphony, appears in his aesthetics as a complex, sophisticated thinker, whose efforts to use Kant's system to answer his own questions — for example, on the beautiful, the sublime, and the future of modern poetry — have been both summarily dismissed and uncritically adulated, seen both as a flight from the political and social problems of his day and as an attempt to engage with them. This study, which is part of the series *Literary Criticism in Perspective*, attempts to trace the history of these extreme divergences in such a way as to cast light on the changing preoccupations and prejudices that gave rise to them as well as on the hidden Schiller himself.

The scope of this investigation has to be defined. The core of aesthetic writings under consideration is made up of the Kallias letters (1793; first translated as part of *Correspondence of Schiller with Körner*, 1849), *Über Anmut und Würde* (1793; translated as *On Grace and Dignity*, 1861), *Über die ästhetische Erziehung des Menschen in einer Reihe von Briefen* (1795; henceforth referred to as *Ästhetische Briefe*; first translated as *On the Aesthetic Education of Man*, 1844), *Über naive und sentimentalische Dichtung* (1795–96; first translated as *On Naive and Sentimental Poetry*, 1861), and *Über das Erhabene* (1801; first translated as *On the Sublime*, 1861), works all written in the period 1793 to 1796. These are the theoretical works that have received the most consistent critical attention and which can properly be called aesthetics. In addition, Schiller wrote a few short pieces on specific issues in aesthetics, a number of essays on tragedy and the theater, essays on the philosophy of history and some pieces of literary criticism on works by other writers. All of these have a bearing on the core of aesthetic writings. To have included these texts in the main discussion would, however, have made the book twice as long and the discussion confusingly dispersed, as these works, unlike the central group, have been the subject of sporadic rather than consistent critical examination. There is also a body of criticism dealing with the relation of various concepts in the aesthetic writings to Schiller's dramas and, to a lesser extent, to his poetry. These essays make more sense in the context of a discussion of the particular dramas or poems, and so I have also excluded them.

Even concentrating on the core of texts, I was not able to discuss every piece of criticism. Readers may find it useful to consult the principal Schiller bibliography, that of Wolfgang Vulpius, *Schiller-Bibliographie 1893–1958* (Weimar: Arion, 1959) and *Schiller-Bibliographie 1959–1963* (Weimar: Aufbau, 1967), supplemented by two further volumes, 1964–1974 (edited by Peter Wersig) and 1975–1985 (edited by Roland Bärwinkel and others). The *Jahrbuch der Deutschen Schillergesellschaft* also produces a bibliographical update every four years or so (see volumes 6, 10, 14, 18, 23, 27, 31, 35), the most recent being that for the period 1987–1990 in vol. 35 (1991). My aim has been to bring to the fore the emphases of the various phases of critical activity, some of which derive from the specific critical and intellectual fashions of the time, others from the sea changes in thought that cause familiar material to assume new relevance or reveal a new aspect. All criticism mentioned in the study is listed in chronological order in the bibliography. The *Ästhetische Briefe* and *Über naive und sentimentalische Dichtung*, Schiller's best-known essays on aesthetics outside the German-speaking world, have occasionally been the subject of strikingly original and illuminating pieces of criticism from commentators outside the fields of German studies and philosophy. One of my aims in this book was to survey material from the broadest range of sources, in order to give Germanists a fuller picture of the material available and non-Germanists access to the debates that have persistently claimed the attention of German-speaking critics. Where a foreign-language study exists in English translation (for example Jung's *Psychological Types*) I have quoted from the published translation, which is listed in the bibliography. Where no published translation exists the translation given here is my own.

In surveying the many works of criticism I have tried to draw attention to what seems to me to be of lasting value. Critics of Schiller's aesthetics tend to belong to one of two camps: those who see the *Ästhetische Briefe* as the pinnacle of Schiller's achievement in aesthetics and the emphasis in that work on the notion of harmony as most representative of his mature thought; and those who see Schiller's aesthetics as the exploration of problems to which he found only partial and temporary solutions and who, therefore, believe that the shifting emphases from one work to another reveal more than does any single work. My sympathies lie more with the latter approach as bringing to light more of the dynamic of Schiller's thought and accounting better for the tensions within individual works. I have, however, tried to be just and objective.

Introduction: The Aesthetic Essays in Outline

SCHILLER'S AESTHETIC ESSAYS were written primarily between 1792 and 1796. They form part of the body of work he produced during the ten-year interval between his two phases of dramatic writing. He burst onto the literary scene in Germany in 1781 with his first play, *Die Räuber* [*The Robbers*], the première of which in 1782 was a theatrical sensation and made him famous. By 1787 he had completed three more plays (*Die Verschwörung des Fiesco zu Genua* [*The Conspiracy of Fiesco in Genoa*], *Kabale und Liebe* [*Intrigue and Love*], and *Don Carlos*), but although he was still convinced that his greatest achievement would lie in the field of drama, he experienced a creative crisis that caused him to turn to nonimaginative writing — historiography, philosophy and aesthetics — in part as a means of reaching greater theoretical clarity about the nature of art and the role of the artist.

Schiller's aesthetic essays are the product of his attempt to discuss some of the central problems of aesthetics in the way that his experience as an artist and his own disposition made him pose them. The questions that repeatedly claimed his attention were the function and status of the aesthetic in human experience and its relation to our freedom as morally autonomous beings. He wanted to show that art and aesthetic experience were fundamental to what it is to be human. The critical apparatus he used in many of his efforts to do so was that of Kant's philosophy, the most up-to-date available to him, although the nature and extent of Kant's influence on him and the legitimacy of his attempts to extend the scope of Kant's terms and method are, as this study shows, still matters of dispute. In 1789 he took up a professorship at the University of Jena offered to him on the basis of his *Geschichte des Abfalls der Niederlande* (*History of the Revolt of the Netherlands*). In 1791 his health broke down, and he decided to use the three-year pension he was given by Danish admirers to pursue a serious study of Kant's philosophy, beginning with the *Kritik der Urteilskraft* [*Critique of Judgment*], which had appeared in 1790. In the *Critique of Judgment* Kant had established that aesthetic judgment was distinct from cognitive or moral judgment, and had hinted that the aesthetic is a kind of bridge linking our experience as members of the realm of nature and our experience as members of the realm of free moral self-determination. Schiller's aesthetic essays offer a number of approaches to the problem of defining beauty in such a way as to maintain its distinctness from other forms of judgment and yet to show its relationship to ethics. This purpose is the thread that runs through the Kallias letters, *Über Anmut und Würde* and the *Ästhetische Briefe*. Also running through all of them is Schiller's preoccupation with freedom, a concern that long predated his study of Kant and that accounts for the enthusiasm with which he responded to Kant. Schiller was deeply conscious from his earliest writings of the tension between the sensuous and the moral in human beings. Kant's epistemological discriminations between the phenomenal and the noumenal realms — the realm of nature and the realm of freedom — in his three great critiques tend to be transmuted by Schiller into experiential conflicts in the individual, in which the possibility of exercising freedom is at stake.

The first challenge was that of defining the beautiful. Kant had denied that an objective definition of beauty was possible. Schiller decided to embark on a philosophical dialogue, to be named *Kallias*, to prove that such a definition was possible. The work was never written, but the preparatory letters, written in 1793, in which Schiller discussed the project with his friend Christian Gottfried Körner, shed fascinating light on his thoughts at the time. He was searching for a definition of the beautiful which would unite the sensuous and the rational and he came up with his famous formulation that beauty is "Freiheit in der Erscheinung" (freedom in appearance/visible form). He means that a beautiful object strikes the beholder as being self-determining or detached from the compulsion that normally governs objects in the phenomenal world. That object thus serves as a symbol of freedom, in the sense of autonomy or moral self-determination, though it shows freedom only in appearance, since all objects in the phenomenal world are subject to the laws of nature. Though the project was abandoned, the Kallias letters provide us with some of the essentials of Schiller's approach.

Über Anmut und Würde, written in 1793, is an exploration of the relationship between the aesthetic and the moral in human beings. Grace is the product of beauty in movement. Moral grace is the apparently instinctive and effortless harmony of sensuous impulse and moral precept and is exhibited above all by the "schöne Seele" (beautiful soul), a term current in the eighteenth century and appropriated by Schiller for his argument. Dignity is the product of individual acts of obedience to the moral law when those acts are the result of conflict between duty and natural impulse. In this essay Schiller moves towards a concept of beauty which embraces the beautiful and the sublime, the terms *grace* and *dignity* being cognate with the beautiful and the sub-lime, respectively. The later part of the eighteenth century saw an up-surge in interest in the sublime as an aesthetic phenomenon related to but distinct from the beautiful. The sublime was held to inspire a mixed response, of pain or terror along with pleasure, whereas the beautiful was associated with harmony. Schiller's aesthetics are, among other things, an ambitious attempt to develop a theory of beauty that also embraces the sublime and, thus, a theory that comprehends all art forms, both those tending toward the soothing effect of beauty and those tending toward the more bracing effect of the sublime. As a tra-gedian he was drawn to an art form that, like the sublime, provokes a mixed response: serenity is achieved through pity and fear. Building on Kant's discussion of the sublime in the *Critique of Judgment*, he saw the sublime as a point of coincidence of the moral and the aesthetic, for the effect of the sublime rests on the assertion of moral freedom. Na-ture, whether in the form of external forces or of our own sensuous being, threatens to overwhelm our freedom. Our humanity is saved when we realize that as rational beings we belong to the intelligible world and need not be overwhelmed by the forces of nature. In *Über Anmut und Würde* Schiller attempts a synthesis of the beautiful and the sublime by postulating the need for the beautiful soul, when under pressure, to evince dignity. Grace and dignity should, thus, alternate in the same person. This attempt to synthesize two arguably incompatible models, with the resulting logical problems, occurs again in the *Ästhe-tische Briefe* and in *Über naive und sentimentalische Dichtung*.

The essay that defines most clearly Schiller's view of the sublime in tragedy is *Über das Pathetische* (1793; translated as *On the Pathetic*, 1861). Two earlier essays, *Über den Grund des Vergnügens an tra-gischen Gegenständen* (1792; translated as *On the Reason for Taking Pleasure in Tragic Subjects*, 1861) and *Über die tragische Kunst* (1792; translated as *On the Art of Tragedy*, 1861), predate his serious study of Kant. In *Über das Pathetische* he discusses the usability of the sublime of moral transcendence in tragedy, making a clear distinction between what we find morally worthy and what we find aesthetically pleasing. Schiller's description of the effect of tragedy in that essay may be re-garded as a way of redefining catharsis by means of a concept of the sublime. It has had a problematic afterlife, in that critics who wish to tie Schiller's dramatic practice closely to his theoretical pronouncements have sometimes applied it too rigidly, while its place within the devel-opment of Schiller's thinking on the sublime has not been fully ex-plored.

Über die ästhetische Erziehung des Menschen in einer Reihe von Briefen (1794), often referred to simply as the *Ästhetische Briefe* [Aesthetic Letters], is Schiller's most famous and certainly his most-discussed work on aesthetics. It combines a theory of art with an analysis of the ills of modern society and shows Schiller grappling with the problem of why the French Revolution, though based on principles of reason, had led so quickly to a new tyranny. The division of the modern being into heart and head, the fragmentation caused by increasing specialization, can be healed only if, through aesthetic education, human beings can reestablish wholeness within themselves. Schiller's transcendental deduction of beauty aims to show art as indispensable to being human. Just as the individual is made up of matter and form (the Aristotelian echoes are clear here) and must achieve a balance between the two fundamental impulses — toward sensuous experience, on the one hand, and integration and control, on the other — so art itself is composed of an interpenetration of matter and form, to which Schiller gives the name *lebende Gestalt* [living form]. Mediating between the two basic impulses is what Schiller calls the *Spieltrieb* [play impulse], the impulse that causes us to take pleasure in the beautiful. The notion of aesthetic education involves the paradox that only when art is recognized as serving no purpose whatsoever can it work on us in its unique way, reestablishing our lost harmony. Art achieves this effect by taking us back to an indeterminate state where, briefly, we experience wholeness again. An indispensable element in this process is what Schiller calls *Schein*, usually translated as *illusion* or *semblance*. This is the quality of the work of art when viewed as an aesthetic object, a quality of detachment from other objects not viewed aesthetically. The *Ästhetische Briefe* are a fragment. They begin with the ideal of the State of Reason, which is characterized by right thinking expressed in right doing, and end with the evocation of the Aesthetic State, in which all members cultivate an aesthetic attitude. Schiller asks in the final paragraph whether such a state exists. This most overtly political of Schiller's aesthetic essays has aroused repeated controversy not least because of the difficulty of reconciling the end with the beginning.

The *Ästhetische Briefe* provide another example of Schiller's attempt to combine the sublime and the beautiful, in this case in his notions of *schmelzende Schönheit* [melting beauty] and *energische Schönheit* [energetic beauty]. The attempt remains incomplete, however, for he delivers a full account only of melting beauty. He turned his attention to the sublime again in the short essay *Über das Erhabene* [*On the Sublime*], published only in 1801 though dating most probably from the period 1794 to 1795. This essay, often taken to be the account of energetic beauty missing from the *Ästhetische Briefe*, is arguably incompatible with that work. It starts from the premise that the world is chaos, not susceptible to the influence of reason. The world of natural forces constantly tries to defeat human beings, who must resist with the power of their consciousness that they belong to the intelligible world. Beauty itself, being part of the sensuous world, can ensnare us, and only the sublime can raise us above the material world. It is Schiller's repeated tendency to undermine models he has set up himself that makes his aesthetic essays so baffling. Yet, on the other hand, the very dynamics of those essays reflect the restless intellect of their author.

Über naive und sentimentalische Dichtung (1795) is perhaps the best-known title of any of Schiller's aesthetic essays outside the German-speaking world. That title is a problem for the translator. *Naive* and *sentimental* are apparently familiar terms which Schiller endows with his own particular meanings. *Dichtung* means imaginative writing with some literary pretentions — in other words, poetry in the broad sense. Although the *Ästhetische Briefe* have claimed the greatest amount of critical attention, this essay, the extent of whose influence has never been properly appreciated, may be his greatest theoretical work. In his essay "Goethe und Tolstoi" Thomas Mann called it "the classical and comprehensive essay of the Germans which actually contains all others and renders them superfluous." (1960, 61)It is a typology of literature that suggests that all writers can be divided into those who are able to depict external reality directly, without interposing their personality between the reader and the material (the naive) and those who reflect on their material and thus color their depiction of reality with their viewpoint and personality (the sentimental). This typology corresponds only partially to the old distinction between ancient and modern poetry. Schiller's aim is to vindicate the modern, sentimental poet, the kind of poet he felt himself to be. The essay was written, in part at least, as a way of accounting for the difference between his poetic consciousness and Goethe's. After some years of distant acquaintance the two men, whose literary aims gave them so much in common, forged a close alliance which lasted until Schiller's death in 1805 and was of immeasurable influence in the development of German letters. Schiller saw in Goethe a contemporary who retained something of the quality of directness of the naive poet. Yet, although he associates the naive poet with the ancient world and the sentimental with the characteristically divided consciousness of people in the modern world, in the course of his argument he moves away from positing an absolute dis-

tinction in poetic consciousness toward a recognition of their reciproc-
ity and ends by postulating a higher reconciliation that unites the best
features of both types of poetry. This maneuver is reminiscent of his
attempts earlier to unite the beautiful and the sublime, grace and dignity; and certainly the naive and the sentimental are related to the
equivalent terms in those other two antithetical pairs. Schiller was no
longer attempting to bring his argument within a rigorously constructed philosophical framework, and the essay consequently shows
numerous shifts of focus and in the meaning of terms. Yet it is characterized by the intense honesty of his self-scrutiny as well as by his longing to transcend his own poetic limitations. *Über naive und sentimentalische Dichtung* helped build a bridge for Schiller back to poetic work.
After it he turned away decisively from theoretical speculation.

1. The First Half-Century

THE STORY OF the critical reception of Schiller's aesthetic writings in the first three decades after they were written is brief but instructive: after the first reactions to their publication they were almost completely ignored. The reasons are not hard to find. Then, as now, there was only a small readership for essays on aesthetics. Schiller's essays were generally assumed to be difficult and obscure, and few general readers were going to give themselves the trouble of struggling with them. Literary scholarship as an academic discipline did not yet exist, and even if it had existed it was only with the benefit of a half-century's hindsight that critics could see the place these essays occupied in eighteenth-century debates and the contribution they had made to the development of aesthetics. The period up to the middle of the nineteenth century, in spite of the relative paucity of material, is nevertheless indicative of certain influential and longstanding tendencies in Schiller scholarship, in particular that of harnessing Schiller's works to serve contemporary political goals. While this characterization is overwhelmingly true of the reception of the plays in this period, the tendency is also clear in the reception of Schiller's aesthetics, and it is not surprising to find that the *Ästhetische Briefe*, the most clearly political of the aesthetic essays, dominate the critical literature.

This neglect of his aesthetic writings did not derive from a general neglect of Schiller but rather from the opposite: a saturation of the public with his popular image. But, as Norbert Oellers notes in his review of Schiller reception up to 1832, that abundance of material was not characterized by its profundity (1967, 274). The impetus for much of the Schiller literature of this period came not from serious engagement with his works but from the opportunity to profit from the cult of Schiller that was developing before his death. Schiller's status as a great writer and as an exemplary German was taken for granted, his admirers were legion, and there was immense public interest in the details of his biography. In the first years after his death a mass of anecdotal biographies and memoirs appeared, many containing invented stories that continued to circulate at least until the middle of the nineteenth century. The very familiarity of so many of Schiller's poetic works stood in the way of sustained inquiry into his philosophical concerns and the development of his thought.

Virtually all of Schiller's aesthetic essays appeared first between 1792 and 1796 in one of two journals edited by him, the *Neue Thalia* or *Die Horen*. The exceptions were *Über das Erhabene* and *Gedanken über den Gebrauch des Gemeinen und Niedrigen in der Kunst* [Thoughts on the Use of Common and Lowly Elements in Art], which were first published in the collection *Kleinere prosaische Schriften* in 1801 and 1802. The two major essays on aesthetics, *Briefe über die ästhetische Erziehung des Menschen* and *Über naive und sentimentalische Dichtung* each appeared in three parts in *Die Horen*. This method of publication meant that, by comparison with the appearance of a play or a collection of poems, contemporary critical reaction was dispersed and, in the case of the shorter essays, muted. The work that provoked the liveliest response from critics on publication was the *Ästhetische Briefe*, in part because it was caught up in the general controversy surrounding *Die Horen*. Schiller had stressed when announcing the new journal that it was to present matters of cultural interest in a manner accessible to the educated lay person and to avoid the purely scientific, religious, or political. The status of the editor and the formidable group of collaborators, including Goethe, Fichte, and Wilhelm von Humboldt, made the project a target of criticism for anyone who did not sympathize with it. The underlying aim — to raise public taste by offering contributions of high quality — seemed to many to be an attempt by Schiller and Goethe to impose their own alien and elitist standards. Published reviews of the *Ästhetische Briefe* were mainly negative. The complimentary review (1795) of the first nine letters by Christian Gottfried Schütz, editor of the *Allgemeine Literatur-Zeitung* (quoted in Fambach 1957, 104–111), which praised their clarity, precision, and elegance, itself attracted much hostile criticism. The (to some, unwarranted) length of the review was noted, and the fact that Schiller had unwisely negotiated for a long and speedy review to be published at the expense of Cotta, publisher of *Die Horen*, seemed to many to undermine the independence of the *Allgemeine Literatur-Zeitung*. Johann Kaspar Friedrich Manso, a rationalist critic, and Friedrich August Mackensen, a Kantian, writing in 1795 in the *Neue Bibliothek der schönen Wissenschaften und der freyen Künste* and *Annalen der Philosophie und des philosophischen Geistes*, respectively (quoted in Fambach 1957, 126–145; 151–167), criticize Schiller's allegedly obscure language and resent his adaptation of Kantian terminology to suit his argument. They were the first of a series of critics who dismissed Schiller's philosophizing as vitiated by poetic language and as making incorrect use of Kantian categories. The arguments of the letters were left almost untouched by the reviewers.

Mackensen rejects the idea of a link between moral freedom and aesthetic experience as "abentheuerlich" [eccentric] Manso, a classical expert, criticizes — with some justification — Schiller's idealization of Ancient Greece but in so doing overlooks its function within the argument. Friedrich Nicolai, the archrationalist Berlin publisher and author, devoted over sixty pages of volume 11 of his *Beschreibung einer Reise durch Deutschland und die Schweiz* [Description of a Journey through Germany and Switzerland, 1796] to criticism of the journal and its impenetrable contributions. Stung, no doubt, by Schiller's view in the letters that purely rational enlightenment had failed, Nicolai expends a good deal of satirical energy on them, claiming that the work is in danger of turning the heads of the young by its suggestion that if people only join their *Sachtrieb* (Schiller's original term for the *Stofftrieb*, [the material impulse]) to their *Formtrieb* [form impulse] they can exhibit *reine Vernunft* [pure reason] and so make the state superfluous. Underlying Nicolai's comic exaggeration is the fact that he has grasped the potentially radical political import of the treatise and is alarmed by it. The frequent incomprehension the work met emerges clearly in private letters by contemporaries, both by the potentially well-disposed such as the *Popularphilosoph* Christian Garve (quoted in Fambach 1957, 168) as well as by the overtly hostile such as Friedrich Schlegel (1890, 235). In particular, we find a widespread echoing of Manso's and Mackensen's distrust of Schiller's attempt to combine Kantian principles with his own terminology, poetic language, and rhetoric. This view of his aesthetic writings as a whole became entrenched in the following years. Georg Gustav Fülleborn suggests that for all their genius the essays' mixture of poetry, Kant, and Fichte can appeal to few readers (1801, 43). Eighteen years later Friedrich Bouterwek, the anti-Romantic professor from Göttingen, admires the brilliant intellectual content of the essays and the "magic of their style" but claims that the truth is often lost amid the dazzling use of language (1819, 420).

The wave of negative criticism that broke over *Die Horen* at the time the *Ästhetische Briefe* appeared had subsided somewhat by the time of the publication of *Über naive und sentimentalische Dichtung* the following year, and there is little published contemporary public comment on the essay. Yet there is no doubt that Schiller's distinction, coming at a time of renewed speculation about the comparative merits of ancient and modern literature, struck a contemporary chord, as Goethe's familiar recollection to Johann Peter Eckermann confirms:

Der Begriff von klassischer und romantischer Poesie, die jetzt über die ganze Welt geht und soviel Streit und Spaltungen verursacht, fuhr Goethe fort, ist ursprünglich von mir und Schiller ausgegangen. Ich hatte in der Poesie die Maxime des objektiven Verfahrens und wollte nur dieses gelten lassen, Schiller aber, der ganz subjektiv wirkte, hielt seine Art für die rechte, und um sich gegen mich zu wehren, schrieb er den Aufsatz über naive und sentimentalische Dichtung (Eckermann 1836, 367).

[The concept of classical and romantic poetry, which is now spreading all over the world and causing so much conflict and division, Goethe continued, originated with me and Schiller. In poetry I was guided by principles of objectivity and wanted to recognise this method only. Schiller, however, whose method was wholly subjective, maintained his way was the right one, and in order to defend himself against me he wrote the essay about naive and sentimental poetry.]

This statement is misleading in more ways than one. For one thing, in their Schillerian definition the terms *naive* and *sentimental* do not correspond to *classical* and *romantic*. Goethe's comment also lends support to another widespread oversimplification: that the essay's main impetus came from Schiller's desire to assert his type of poetic consciousness against Goethe's. Schiller does not consider either type to be "the right one," and far from being overawed by the naive poet he is so successful at vindicating the sentimental one that the naive is left looking rather threadbare. Also, of course, Goethe does not mention the essay's reworking of important themes in Schiller's other theoretical essays. Yet the very fact that Goethe runs together the pairs *naive-sentimental* and *classical-romantic* indicates how quickly Schiller's distinction was adapted by Romantic critics and became part of people's mental furniture.

In spite of the importance of the essay in providing an impetus for the crystallization of Romantic criticism, the Romantics, in accordance with their policy of elevating Goethe and keeping a telling silence on Schiller, say little directly about it. One of the few comments by August Wilhelm Schlegel is in his *Geschichte der klassischen Litteratur* [History of Classical Literature, 1802–3] but it is quite oblique. It is provoked by Schiller's suggestion that Euripides shows traces of the sentimental poet:

Überhaupt reicht man mit dieser Eintheilung in der Geschichte der Poesie nicht weit: es sind Verhältnisbegriffe aus dem subjektiven Standpunkt der Sentimentalität, die außer dem keine Realität haben: denn für wen ist denn das sogenannte Naive naiv, außer für den Sentimentalen? . . . Den Shakspeare aber, der ein Abgrund von Absichtlichkeit, Selbstbewußtsein und Reflexion ist, für einen naiven Dichter, den materiellen sinnlichen Ariost hingegen für einen sentimentalen zu erklären, scheint eine große Naivetät zu seyn.(375–76)

[In any case this classification in the history of poetry does not get one very far. They are relative concepts derived from the subjective standpoint of the sentimental condition which have no reality apart from it. For for whom is the so-called naive naive, except for the sentimental person? . . . However, to call Shakespeare, who is an abyss of deliberateness, self-consciousness and reflectiveness, a naive poet, and yet to call the materially minded, sensuous Ariosto a sentimental one seems extremely naive.]

The Romantics were bound to quarrel with Schiller's views of various authors because for them Shakespeare and Goethe were the "romantic" poets *par excellence*, whereas Schiller had placed them (though not unproblematically) in the naive category. Schlegel distances himself from Schiller's typology by using the German word *sentimental* instead of *sentimentalisch*, which is Schiller's term and one to which the essay gives a specialized meaning. He also exaggerates the extent to which the naive-sentimental distinction is a historical one. Jean Paul (Richter), at first an admirer of Schiller until tensions entered their relations, speaks only briefly and slightingly of *Über naive und sentimentalische Dichtung* in sections 21 and 22 of his *Vorschule der Ästhetik* [Preliminaries of Aesthetics, 1804]. Like August Wilhelm Schlegel he objects to Schiller's classification of specific writers as naive or sentimental (he too refuses to use Schiller's word *sentimentalisch*) and overstresses the historical nature of the division. Like Herder, toward whose aesthetic ideas he felt a greater sympathy, he doubts the usefulness of any such sweeping distinction. Schiller's identification of the question of the self-consciousness of the artist, an issue so important in Romantic criticism, is ignored by both Schlegel and Jean Paul.

During the controversies over *Die Horen* Schiller learned that a person who was one of his supporters, but a rather indifferent critic, was planning a public defense of the journal. Schiller was more perturbed about that prospect than about the possibility of negative criticism from some of his opponents. He wrote to Goethe that it was a particular misfortune that, surrounded as he was by so many vociferous enemies, he had to silence one of the few voices speaking up for him. In the years following his death Schiller's enemies grew fewer; even those as bitter as Friedrich Schlegel seem in later years to have been willing to give him some praise. The number of his uncomprehending admirers

grew, however, and from them he had more to fear than from his opponents, for they successfully stifled any urge that may have arisen to
look beyond the popular image. It was not until the 1820s that there
was impetus to deepen and make more intellectually coherent the appreciation of Schiller's achievement and so prepare the way for an
evaluation of his aesthetic writings. Here the two key figures are Georg
Wilhelm Friedrich Hegel and Wilhelm von Humboldt. Although neither discusses any individual work in any detail, both were concerned
that Schiller's intellectual achievement should be seen in its distinctive-
ness and not be overshadowed by Kant and Goethe.

Hegel was always an ardent admirer of Schiller. As a young man he
greeted the appearance of the first section of the *Ästhetische Briefe* with
enthusiasm. Between 1818 and 1828 he delivered his lectures on aesthetics at least five times at the University of Berlin. In the posthu-
mously published version of those lectures he sums up Schiller's
contribution in this field:

> Es muß *Schillern* das große Verdienst zugestanden werden, die kan-
> tische Subjektivität und Abstraction des Denkens durchbrochen und
> den Versuch gewagt zu haben, über sie hinaus die Einheit und Ver-
> söhnung denkend als das Wahre zu fassen und künstlerisch zu ver-
> wirklichen (1835, 1838, I, 101).

> [*Schiller* must be accorded the great merit of having broken through
> the subjectivity and abstraction of Kant's thought and having dared to
> think beyond them, grasping unity and reconciliation as objective
> truth and realizing them in art.]

Kant is, for Hegel, a key figure in the development of the understanding of the beautiful in art ("das Kunstschöne"), for Kant saw that in
aesthetic judgment there is a uniting of faculties that are normally distinct. Kant's system could not, however, allow him to postulate that
reconciliation outside the individual subject. Schiller showed the way
forward in aesthetics by accomplishing that leap from the subjective to
the objective idea of beauty and thus led on to Schelling. Moreover,
Hegel vindicates Schiller's activity as a thinker in the face of objections
that he tried to combine philosophy and poetry. He commends him for
placing his considerations of the nature of art within a philosophical
framework rather than solely in that of his immediate practical concerns
as an artist. Thus, his results, whatever harm may have been done to his
poetry, have the merit of spanning the fields of literature and philosophy. Hegel's vindication of Schiller is an explicit reply to those who see
Goethe's poetic work as untrammeled by philosophy. He points out

that Goethe turned to studying the natural sciences and, thus, manifests the same need to broaden and enrich his intellectual pursuits. He discusses only the *Ästhetische Briefe* as an individual work and then only briefly, concentrating on the link Schiller develops between aesthetic education and the renewal of the state. His lectures, however, established Schiller as vital figure in the history of aesthetics and gave impetus to his pupils to look for the intellectual coherence in his work. This search, of course, led to distortions and forced readings, especially of the plays , but these were a sign of deeper engagement and a welcome break from the moralistic admiration more typical of the period.

Wilhelm von Humboldt, the Prussian lawyer, diplomat, and educational reformer, became a close friend of Schiller's in the mid-1790s and conducted an extensive correspondence with him. In 1830 Humboldt edited and published this correspondence, prefacing it with an essay entitled "Über Schiller und den Gang seiner Geistesentwicklung" [On Schiller and the Course of His Intellectual Development]. The main years of the correspondence, 1793 to 1797, cover the period when Schiller was chiefly engaged with aesthetics but was also moving back toward drama and poetry. The Goethe-Schiller correspondence, which had been published in 1828 and 1829, also begins in the years of Schiller's philosophical activity, but Schiller did not find in Goethe a partner to share his speculative concerns and thus the correspondence did not throw much light on his aesthetic writings. Humboldt does not analyze any of the individual works in detail in his essay. His aim, as the title suggests, is to stress the coherence and unity of Schiller's achievement as poet *and* thinker. Humboldt contends that the central years of their correspondence show that poetry and philosophy occupied Schiller's entire mind, and that his intellectual energy was directed toward investigating and presenting their common origin. One cannot, therefore, understand Schiller's work piecemeal. Humboldt is concerned to dispel the prejudice that one cannot be both poet and philosopher. He is also at pains to make clear that Schiller, though obviously influenced by Kant and Goethe, was never enslaved to any other poet or thinker but knew how to use the impetus he received from contact with other significant figures to stimulate his own work. Humboldt was the first commentator to point out that the seeds of much of Schiller's thought of the Kantian period can be found in his work of the 1780s, an insight that took several decades to come to fruition in Schiller scholarship. The letters themselves shed much light on the relation between poetry and philosophy in Schiller's work. The reader, however, finds also that they reflect a much greater unease on Schiller's part with his two vocations than Humboldt suggests in his essay. Humboldt's aim is to see his friend's intellectual achievement properly appreciated rather than to expose its problematic aspects.

The dominant trend in Schiller appreciation in the 1820s is summed up in the work of Wolfgang Menzel. In Menzel's *Die deutsche Literatur* [German Literature](1828) an idealized Schiller replaces serious engagement with his work. For Menzel the poet and his work were all of a piece. Schillerian characters are ideal beings who represent the highest moral beauty and sublimity. Menzel approves of Schiller because the latter was able combine artistic merit with moral uplift. The aesthetic essays receive no mention at all. Menzel's approach to Schiller is also typical of the 1820s insofar as he sets Schiller against Goethe. The need to take sides stretches back to the feuds and animosities of the 1790s, when the Jena Romantics elevated Goethe and ignored Schiller. Menzel particularly disapproved of Goethe's immorality and lack of commitment to religion or to his country. Schiller, by contrast, is the moral mentor of the nation and speaks directly to the people through his works. Menzel's history was immensely successful, and its success helps the present-day observer to understand why it was so difficult to find serious discussion of Schiller's aesthetics. Not only was the image fixed, but it was increasingly harnessed to political allegiances.

Menzel's excesses did, however, provoke a reaction (well documented by Delinière 1977). Writers of a more radical turn of mind, including the writers of "Das Junge Deutschland" [Young Germany], were stirred to offer their own appraisals of Goethe and Schiller; and although there was among these writers greater appreciation of Goethe, they reacted against the moralistic and partisan playing off of one against the other. The death of Goethe in 1832 in any case seemed to many the end of an epoch and an appropriate time to assess the greats of Weimar. Amongst the writings of the Jungdeutschen [Young Germans] we catch glimpses of an awareness of Schiller's aesthetics, but although reacting against Menzel, they nevertheless filter all their views through their own political lens. Ludolf Wienbarg's *Ästhetische Feldzüge* [Aesthetic Campaigns], the most influential theoretical statement of the Jungdeutschen, put forward the rather eccentric view that Kant's aesthetics were now only of antiquarian interest; Schiller was led astray by his admiration for Kant into aesthetic speculation, which only caused him mental conflict. Wienbarg also complains that Schiller's dramas (unlike Goethe's — another surprising judgment) are not organically linked to their age but are products of the desire to produce a certain kind of art. Wienbarg wanted to see writers in critical engagement with the era and felt that in turning to aesthetics Schiller was wasting his energy on an obsolete concern. A more sympathetic but equally superficial appraisal is found in the work of Heinrich Laube, another of the Jungdeutschen. In his *Geschichte der deutschen Literatur* [History of German Literature], published in four volumes in 1839 and 1840, Laube rallies to the defense of Schiller's aesthetic essays as serious works and not just the products of a dilettante philosopher, attributing their neglect to the Romantics' dismissal of their author. Laube's own summary of the *Ästhetische Briefe* would not, however, have pleased their author. The state, he claims, no longer knows how to use people in their totality; only create more human beings in the light of this artistic ideal and thus establish a new state. This gross oversimplification of the text and disregard for its problematic presentation of the relation between political means and ends is the result of Laube's wish to harness it for liberal purposes. Heine's appraisal of Schiller's aesthetics is confined to a few lines in *Zur Geschichte der Religion und Philosophie in Deutschland* [On the History of Religion and Philosophy in Germany] (1835), where he calls Schiller "ein gewaltsamer Kantianer" [a Kantian with a vengeance] and asserts that Kantian philosophy in its dry abstraction was detrimental to art and literature.

For the Junghegelianer [Young Hegelians] of the left Schiller occupied a key position as prophet of a better world. In 1839 and 1840 *Der Protestantismus und die Romantik* [Protestantism and Romanticism], a famously controversial work, was published in installments in the *Hallische Jahrbücher für deutsche Wissenschaft und Kunst*, the repository of ideas of the Junghegelianer. The authors, Theodor Echtermeyer and Arnold Ruge, the radical liberal publicist and associate of Karl Marx, expounded the view that Romanticism had been a movement of intellectual aristocracy, overturning the leveling and rational tendencies of the Enlightenment. In this scheme Schiller's notion of art's reconciling function marks him out as a prophet of humanity, anticipating, as an abstract ideal if not in political reality, the renewal of the state and emancipation of the individual for which they hoped. Here again we see Schiller caught up in the reaction against Romanticism and the conservative nationalism associated with that movement.

The three most serious engagements with Schiller's aesthetics in the late 1830s and early 1840s came from Karl Hoffmeister, Georg Gottfried Gervinus, and Karl Grün, writers who were quite different in approach but who all made an attempt to see Schiller's life, work, and thought as a coherent whole. Hoffmeister's title, *Schillers Leben, Geistes-*

entwickelung und Werke im Zusammenhang [Schiller's Life, Intellectual Development and Works 'in Relation to Each Other] (1838–42), indicates his aim to take a strongly biographical approach free from political ax-grinding. The work is a monumental achievement and gave the lead in creating a Schiller criticism based on thorough research, as far as the availability of material allowed. Hoffmeister's attempt at building up a coherent picture of Schiller's intellectual development may be seen as a fulfillment of the impulse given by Wilhelm von Humboldt. Certainly Hoffmeister makes extensive use of the correspondence with Humboldt and with Goethe. He carefully traces the development of the theory of the sublime in Schiller's shorter essays on tragedy in an exposition that is clear and accurate. As a scholar well grounded in Kant, he tends, while expressing admiration for the aesthetic works, to be unsparing in raising objections to them. He realizes, for instance, that Schiller's concern with the sublime and the beautiful makes it difficult for him to formulate any theory of aesthetic experience that embraces both. He recognizes that the treatment of the sublime is missing from the *Ästhetische Briefe* but also that Schiller's account of the Spieltrieb as a harmonizing impulse does not provide a model for the sublime as an aesthetic experience. His comments on *Über naive und sentimentalische Dichtung* raise the logical problem of the exclusion of the sublime from the naive. Because Hoffmeister sees the rich intellectual content of the essays, he praises them; but because he cannot overlook or account for the problems raised by Schiller's characteristic method of arguing, his discussions have the air of damning with faint praise. His strongly biographical approach also leads him to neglect the intellectual and cultural context of the essays (or to take them for granted) and his conviction that science has progressed and made the psychology of the *Ästhetische Briefe* redundant makes him occasionally condescending in tone.

Hoffmeister soon found a vigorous opponent in the shape of the radical Hegelian Karl Grün. Grün's aim in *Friedrich Schiller als Mensch, Geschichtsschreiber, Denker und Dichter* [Friedrich Schiller as Man, Historian, Thinker and Poet] (1844) was to present the coherence of Schiller's thought and work in a way that would be concise and accessible to the reading public. For him, intent as he was on pursuing the central idea of the realization of freedom in Schiller's work, the biographical method of Hoffmeister was nit-picking and pedantic. The virulence of Grün's invective against Hoffmeister mars the book for the modern reader; nevertheless, Grün must be given credit for expounding Schiller's thought in the major essays with vigor and engagement. Following Hegel's lead, Grün sees Schiller's aesthetics, the *Ästhetische Briefe* in particular, as an "overcoming" of Kant. In the process he sacrifices precision and simply sweeps aside the problems both in Schiller's use of Kantian terms and in the structure of his own arguments. Noting that the *Ästhetische Briefe* hover between presenting aesthetic education as the means and as the end of humanity's progress, Grün impatiently declares that it does not matter as long as we all get *somewhere*. The political prejudice is clear in this interpretation of the work and also in Grün's insistence that it represents the pinnacle of Schiller's thought. He therefore regrets but cannot explain the fact that after writing the *Ästhetische Briefe* Schiller slips back into, for Grün, an earlier mode of philosophizing in *Über das Erhabene*. In the interpretation of the *Ästhetische Briefe* Grün does, however, see one vital thing. He recognizes that the person-condition argument about the personality at the heart of the *Ästhetische Briefe* is essentially a metaphysical argument, whereas Hoffmeister had inappropriately seen it as superseded by advances in psychology.

The third contribution of lasting value in this period was made by the great historian Gervinus in the fifth volume of his *Geschichte der deutschen Dichtung* [History of German Poetry] (1842, fourth edition, 1853). In the battle between the supporters of Goethe and of Schiller, which was still raging, Gervinus provides a more conciliatory and mediating tone. Combining solid exposition with judicious evaluation, Gervinus tries to see the essays in their historical and literary context and credits Schiller with laying the foundations of an aesthetics based on Kantian principles. His is perhaps the first attempt to look at the aesthetic theories of the eighteenth century in a coherent, historical way. Thus, although he sees Schiller as making free use of Kant, he regards this procedure as a useful supplement to Kant's purely deductive approach, the work of a critic close to literature who could build on Kant's breakthrough but also draw together the work of other thinkers and writers such as Lessing and Herder. Gervinus's liberal tendency is evident in his approach to the *Ästhetische Briefe*; he attributes their being unfinished to the fact that Schiller himself did not live in an age which allowed him to envision the end of aesthetic education in a renewal of the state. Times have changed, however, Gervinus says, and we can now hope for the fulfillment of Schiller's vision — an optimist statement given that Schiller himself talks of aesthetic education as the task of more than one century. While history has proved Gervinus wrong on this point, his exposition of Schein (a central but hitherto neglected aspect of the work) and its relation to imagination in the *Äs-*

thetische Briefe is highly lucid, while in his discussion of *Über naive und sentimentalische Dichtung* he rightly gives prominence to Schiller's critical expertise, rather than dwelling on whether Schiller was right or wrong to call Shakespeare or Goethe naive. Gervinus correctly foresaw that the richness of argument and reference in Schiller's aesthetic essays would make them of interest far beyond the limited fields of aesthetics and literary criticism.

The extent to which the history of the reception of Schiller's aesthetics is distinct both from the history of his popular image and from that of his plays and poetry is emphasized by the almost complete lack of interest shown even by literary people in the appearance in 1847 of Schiller's correspondence with Körner. This correspondence contains, of course, the so-called *Kalliasbriefe*, the letters in which Schiller outlines his ideas for a work on the deduction of beauty and that contain his famous definition of beauty as "Freiheit in der Erscheinung" [freedom in appearance]. The publication of this important section of an important correspondence gave scholars the first opportunity to trace in detail the development of Schiller's engagement with Kant before he worked out the major treatises, while the earlier part of the correspondence shed new light on his intellectual progress in the second half of the 1780s. In 1847, however, people had other preoccupations, and few Schiller enthusiasts were interested in freeing their minds sufficiently from the image of the poet as national icon to appreciate the more challenging facets of his intellect and work as revealed in the correspondence. The exception to the general indifference was Theodor Danzel, a young and highly gifted scholar, whose review essay on the correspondence first appeared in 1848 in the *Wiener Jahrbücher der Literatur*. Danzel's sympathies were much more with Goethe than with Schiller, which may account for his concentration on aesthetics in the review. The correspondence with Körner showed him how far Schiller's basic approach and preoccupations in aesthetics were already evident before he began to read Kant. He realized that the poem "Die Künstler" [The Artists] anticipates the issues Schiller was to treat in the 1790s and he saw Schiller's theorizing as originating in the practical concern to think through his own position. Danzel also recognized the importance of the Kallias letters in making clear the starting point in Schiller's engagement with Kant, namely his interpretation of various key ideas in the *Critique of Judgment*. This recognition leads him to see the *Ästhetische Briefe* as the fulfillment of that original ambition to demonstrate that beauty is "Freiheit in der Erscheinung." Danzel clearly believes that the airy confidence of Hegelian critics that

Schiller had somehow "overcome" Kantian dualism is based on a mis-understanding of Schiller's position. He interprets Schiller as having seen the dualism of mind and nature as absolute and emphasizes the latter's comment that a union of the two is an imperative that cannot actually be realized. Arguably this interpretation is a way of synthesizing Schiller's conflicting positions on this matter. Nevertheless, Danzel's intelligent awareness of the value of the Körner correspondence for the study of Schiller's aesthetics puts his essay on a new plane of sophistica-tion in the Schiller literature and prepares the way for a new generation of studies from the mid-1850s onward.

2. Schiller's Aesthetics Discovered

THE POLITICAL DISAPPOINTMENTS of 1848 silenced Schiller's liberal admirers for a few years, until the 1859 centenary celebrations gave both them and, more especially, patriotic Germans pressing for national unification the chance once more to cast Schiller in their own mold. While up to 1848 the predominating view of Schiller had been that of a champion of progress toward a more liberal political order, in 1859 he had become the cultural icon of the German *Bürgertum* [middle classes]. The educated middle classes saw him as embodying the best German values and viewed his work (increasingly along with Goethe's) as the pinnacle of German cultural achievement. A nation with such a noble cultural heritage should aspire to political unity and assert its place alongside the other nation-states. Schiller's struggle to fulfil his destiny as a writer became a symbol of the nation's struggle for cultural and political recognition. This apotheosis of the popular Schiller contributed next to nothing to the serious study of his plays and poems, and still less to that of his aesthetics.

The 1905 centenary was more subdued and scholarly than the 1859 event, the difference indicating the sea-change that had affected the general response to Schiller. By 1905 he seemed the poet of another age. Yet the second half of the nineteenth century did see the beginning of systematic and serious engagement with Schiller's aesthetics, which issued in two waves of intense activity. As if reacting against the familiarity of Schiller's poems and plays, scholars began to turn their attention to his philosophical, historical, and aesthetic works. Positivist methods of inquiry yielded the first wave, culminating in the first significant collection of studies in the 1860s and the first historical-critical edition, edited by Karl Goedeke, in 1871, while the increasing influence towards the end of the century of Neo-Kantianism brought a new wave of studies up to the time of the 1905 commemoration.

The First Wave

One of those who prepared the way for the first wave was the Jena professor Kuno Fischer. His treatise *Schiller als Philosoph* [Schiller as Philosopher](1858), based on lectures delivered in Jena, is written in an accessible style and, though lightweight, touches on some major issues.

Like Humboldt almost thirty years before, Fischer is at pains to show that an understanding of Schiller's philosophical work is integral to an understanding of his poetic work. He was one of the first critics to turn to Schiller's early philosophy, pointing briefly but suggestively to Platonic and Neo-Platonic influences, and to search in the pre-Kantian writings for ideas that carried through to and crystallized in Schiller's later work after the engagement with Kant. Identifying the unresolved tension between ethics and aesthetics in Schiller's theoretical writings, Fischer constructs a three-stage development: in his early writings Schiller sees the aesthetic as subordinate to the ethical; later it is an equal partner with the ethical; and finally the ethical is subordinate to the aesthetic. This three-stage scheme, which Fischer later repudiated, provoked a good deal of dissent in the following decades. Most scholars challenged his dating of *Über das Erhabene* before the *Ästhetische Briefe*, casting doubt on the notion of such a neat development. Fischer is certainly correct, however, in identifying the uncertain movement between the ethical and the aesthetic and in seeing Schiller as somehow suspicious of his own notion of harmony. Fischer admits that the ending of the *Ästhetische Briefe*, where aesthetic culture seems to have taken precedence over the State of Reason as the end of aesthetic education, poses problems for his theory, but he simply postulates that the aesthetic individual is necessarily moral. Fischer's work could do no more than point the way to more detailed study, but it is indicative of its richness in ideas and lucid style that it was reprinted in 1888 and seemed fresh to a new generation of scholars.

A further short but, in its day, influential study was Wilhelm Hemsen's dissertation *Schiller's Ansichten über Schönheit und Kunst* [Schiller's Views on Beauty and Art](1854). Hemsen sees Schiller moving on from Kant's *Kritik der Urteilskraft* to show the way toward an objective concept of beauty, but as having suffered from a deep ambivalence toward Kant. Schiller, of course, admits to such an ambivalence, which led him to argue in support of him (by adopting his system) and argue against him (as in the deduction of beauty or in his challenge to Kant's moral system in *Über Anmut und Würde*). The result is the sequence of contradictions that confronts us in the aesthetic essays, in particular with regard to the attempted reconciliation of the sublime and the beautiful. Hemsen sees these contradictions as deriving from Schiller's distinctive attitudes rather than from a misunderstanding of Kant: Schiller was constitutionally susceptible to the lure of Kant's dualism but able at times, more by intuition than by logical argument, to reach beyond it. Thus, he achieves true insight in the *Ästhetische*

Briefe into beauty's function in uniting mind and nature and thereby paves the way for Schelling, only to turn away from these insights in *Über das Erhabene.*

In 1862 appeared a work that must be regarded as a landmark in the critical study of Schiller's aesthetic and philosophical writings, Karl Tomaschek's *Schiller in seinem Verhältnisse zur Wissenschaft* [Schiller in His Relationship to Science]. It was written in response to a prize offered on the occasion of the Schiller centenary of 1859 by the Imperial Academy of Sciences in Vienna. In 1857 Tomaschek had published a short but thorough study of Schiller and Kant, and he takes up the results of that study into the larger work. Tomaschek, a professor at the Theresianische Akademie in Vienna, moves impressively through the fields of history, philosophy, and aesthetics with the aim of presenting Schiller's contribution to the development of those fields and gauging what he had achieved that was of lasting significance. For the modern reader Tomaschek's style is very dry and his positivistic approach makes an unimaginative impression; he was frequently criticized by the next generations of scholars for concentrating on the logical errors in Schiller's use of Kant. It is true that Tomaschek has no feel for Schiller's language and little appreciation of his methodological experimentation, and the nit-picking does make it hard to grasp his overall argument. Nevertheless, there is such an argument in his attempt to follow through Schiller's idea of harmony, which leads him to be the first scholar to pay systematic attention to Schiller's early philosophy. Following the lead given by Danzel, he points to the anticipations of Kantian thought in Schiller's correspondence of the late 1780s with Körner. He also shows that Schiller had encountered Kant's essays *Mutmaßlicher Anfang der Menschengeschichte* [Conjectural Beginning of Human History] (1786) and *Idee zu einer Universalgeschichte in weltbürgerlicher Absicht* [Idea for a Universal History with Cosmopolitan Intent] (1784) before his main engagement with Kant's critiques; and he relates these essays not only to Schiller's historical writings but also to the concept of historical development underlying the *Ästhetische Briefe* and *Über naive und sentimentalische Dichtung*: that the progress of the whole produces conflicts in the individual that can ultimately be resolved in the completion of that progress. In discussing the aesthetic essays Tomaschek makes full use of the Kallias letters and the Körner correspondence in general, disagreeing with Danzel that the Kallias project finds its fulfillment in the *Ästhetische Briefe* and seeing instead in that essay the attempt to find a new approach to the deduction of beauty, one that uses Kantian epistemology without falling into the logical problems of the Kallias project.

He gives a convincing account of the divergences between Schiller's thought and Fichte's, rejecting the idea that Schiller's *Triebe* are borrowed from Fichte in spite of a number of similarities in terminology. On *Über naive und sentimentalische Dichtung* Tomaschek is disappointing, and his treatment suggests that he is uninterested in poetics.

A second, less detailed entry for the Vienna Academy competition was the distinguished philosopher Friedrich Überweg's *Schiller als Historiker und Philosoph* [Schiller as Historian and Philosopher], which remained unpublished until 1884. Überweg's particular strengths are his detailed account of Schiller's education and his treatment of the essays on tragedy. In discussing the earlier essays on tragedy he elucidates Schiller's position in relation to Lessing's, correcting Fischer's view that Schiller, like Lessing, abolished Aristotelian fear. On *Über das Pathetische* he attacks the prevalent view that Schiller wished to show guiltless characters and discusses the distinctions Schiller makes between moral and aesthetic responses to tragedy. On the mature aesthetic writings he has less to offer than Tomaschek, though his exposition of the Kallias letters and *Über Anmut und Würde* is sound and clear. On the *Ästhetische Briefe* he espouses the strange notion that Schiller's idea of aesthetic education has been achieved, treating that idea as synonymous with the concept of *Bildung* [education/self-cultivation].

After the pioneering work from Danzel and critics of the 1850s and 1860s, studies of Schiller's aesthetics went through something of a lull. The reasons for this lie partly in a change of intellectual climate and a consequent change in the evaluation of Schiller, and partly in the lull that naturally ensues when a topic seems to have been adequately covered. Although his works still occupied a central position in the cultural pantheon of the *Bildungsbürgertum* [educated middle classes] and no self-respecting educated family was without a set of leather-bound volumes, there was an increasing sense that Schiller was somehow no longer in step with the times. The intellectual climate was shifting toward pessimism, in part under the influence of Arthur Schopenhauer, while in time Friedrich Nietzsche's assaults on the cultural assumptions of his fellow Germans reinforced the feeling that Schiller's idealism and the high-minded rhetoric of his plays and poems belonged to another age. At the same time, Goethe's stock was continually rising. Many critics still showed the partisan tendency to elevate one poet at the expense of the other, and in this period the shift in sympathy toward Goethe was reinforced by the huge expansion of Goethe criticism. The rise of Neo-Kantianism as a countermovement to positivism and materialism, however, ensured that Schiller's aesthetics, at least in so far as they related to Kant, enjoyed renewed attention. In addition, the continued rise of the experimental sciences left their mark on Schiller scholarship, for in the 1890s we see the beginnings of the fascination with Schiller's relation to the empirical tradition. The later decades of the nineteenth century also saw the expansion of the study of German literature as an academic discipline, with the accompanying need for new scholarly studies of major authors.

The Empirical Approach

One of the most fascinating and controversial studies of Schiller produced during this phase is Robert Sommer's *Grundzüge einer Geschichte der deutschen Psychologie und Ästhetik von Wolff-Baumgarten bis Kant-Schiller* [Essentials of a History of German Psychology and Aesthetics from Wolff-Baumgarten to Kant-Schiller](1892), a work based on a treatise written in response to a prize offered by the Berlin Akademie der Wissenschaften on the influence of psychology on the aesthetics of the classical period in German literature. Sommer attempts to provide a counterweight to the studies that concentrate on Kant's influence on Schiller's aesthetics by showing the importance of earlier intellectual influences, particularly that of Gottfried Wilhelm von Leibniz's impact on theories of perception as they came down to Schiller as part of his medical and philosophical studies at the Karlsschule. He argues that Schiller's concern for the organic unity of the whole person is fundamental to his aesthetics and is evident from the early medical writings. This was the first time a scholar had brought his medical writings, *Über den Zusammenhang der tierischen Natur des Menschen mit seiner geistigen* [On the Connection between the Animal and Spiritual Natures of Man] in particular, into direct connection with Schiller's mature aesthetics — an imaginative approach, whatever its dangers. Sommer stresses what he calls Schiller's phenomenalism — the idea that human physical phenomena reflect the human understanding — and sees it as the basis of Schiller's thought before he encountered Kant and refined his conception of subject-object relationships in the light of transcendental idealism. He attempts to reveal the lines of continuity of speculative thought from Leibniz to Kant and the later Enlightenment, while suggesting the provenance of some of Schiller's ideas in the empirical tradition. In laying weight on the organic notion of the human being, he also suggests affinities with the thought of Goethe and Herder. Sommer's aim is to emphasize the organic idea as a countertradition to

Cartesian dualism and he is not alone in picking up on monistic elements in Schiller's early thought. Tomaschek, surprisingly, argues on the basis of next to no evidence for a Spinozan influence in the early treatises. However, while at times Schiller may seem to move toward an organicist position, we have to approach with caution claims of affinity in this matter with Goethe and Herder. Sommer sees Schiller's organicist theory of art as summed up in the phrase *lebende Gestalt*, as used in the *Ästhetische Briefe*. He interprets the phrase as denoting the process by which the response provoked in the subject by an art object is transferred by the mind into the object and seems to represent the "soul" of the object. His discussion of the *Ästhetische Briefe*, for all his fervent admiration for them, is less successful than that of the early philosophy because he drifts into speculative elaboration of Schiller's antitheses. He stresses three points, however, that are of lasting value in the criticism of the work. First, he traces the possible provenance of the notion of a Spieltrieb in the empirical tradition. Second, he elucidates the affinities between Herder's notion of ascending stages in human development in the *Ideen* [Ideas] (1784–91) and Schiller's idea of cultural progression. Third, he suggests the origin of Schiller's notion of Schein in Leibnizian monadology via Lambert. To those who insist on the essentially metaphysical nature of Schiller's theory of beauty the validity of Sommer's approach seems limited. It nevertheless suggests important links between the earlier thought and the mature aesthetics that still require precise investigation. Sommer's book was reprinted in 1975, a time of renewed interest in the anthropological approach to literature and literary theories.

The year after Sommer's study appeared, Karl Gneisse's *Schillers Lehre von der ästhetischen Wahrnehmung* [Schiller's Doctrine of Aesthetic Perception] was published. It met with little approval at the time because it abandoned the philological approach, with Kant as starting point, in favor of interpretation in the light of contemporary theories of perception and thereby provoked, as had Sommer's work, the objection that the metaphysical nature of Schiller's arguments had not been recognized. Gneisse extrapolates from the *Ästhetische Briefe* what Schiller's notion of perception in general, and aesthetic perception in particular, must have been, arguing that for Schiller the distinctions of Kantian metaphysics of knowing, feeling and desiring existed in name only. In the perceiving subject all three are at work. The state of aesthetic perception, which Gneisse defines as a middle state between cognition and feeling, becomes a modulation of the whole psyche, whereas previous commentators had frequently assumed that aesthetic perception was a faculty of the psyche. Gneisse's contention that Schiller saw the psyche as a unity allows him to explain (rather too neatly) the tension in Schiller's aesthetics between the moral and the aesthetic in terms of a tipping of the balance rather than as any fundamental conflict. To that extent Gneisse, in spite of the controversial nature of his approach, fits into the school of critics who approach Schiller's aesthetics with the intention of finding unity and consistency.

Philosophical Approaches

A study that attempts to mediate between the philosophical and psychological approaches to Schiller's aesthetics is Eugen Kühnemann's *Kants und Schillers Begründung der Ästhetik* [The Foundation of Aesthetics in Kant and Schiller] (1895). Though a pupil of the prominent Neo-Kantian Hermann Cohen, Kühnemann diverges from the Neo-Kantian tendency to stress the continuity of Schiller's thought with Kant's. After a compact survey of Kant's approach to aesthetic questions, Kühnemann begins his discussion of Schiller with the primary impulse behind Schiller's aesthetics, which he takes to be the desire to reach clarity in his own mind about his task as an artist. Though Kühnemann devotes the greatest amount of space to the *Ästhetische Briefe*, the most fruitful parts of his discussion are arguably those concerning the Kallias letters, where he clarifies Schiller's relation to Kant, and *Über naive und sentimentalische Dichtung*, where he is one of the first commentators to do more than sketch the argument. He stresses two central pillars in Schiller's reading of Kant — freedom and nature — detaching them from Kant's system and using them as fixed points within which to explore his own preoccupations. Kühnemann recognizes that Kant and Schiller were engaged in different projects, Kant's being primarily epistemological whereas Schiller was concerned to establish the principles of art and his role as an artist. Thus, Kühnemann sees the Kallias project as a creative misunderstanding on Schiller's part. Kant had denied the possibility of an objective principle in aesthetics so as to secure aesthetics its own foundation, distinct from other kinds of knowledge. Schiller mistook that denial for the assertion that aesthetics could have no systematic scientific foundation, whereas Kant was concerned to secure the place of feeling in aesthetic judgment. Thus, in Kühnemann's view, Schiller's Kallias project was bound to lead to nothing. Nevertheless, the notion of "Freiheit in der Erscheinung" led Schiller on to what really interested him: the qualities of art objects, the role of art in human development, and the disposition of the artist. Kühnemann, therefore, takes up a clear standpoint with regard to the question of Schiller's having "overcome" Kant: because of their divergent concerns and emphases, such talk is, for him, entirely misplaced. Kühnemann is less convincing in his emphasis on Schiller as "Psychologe" [psychologist]. Schiller's approach in his Kantian phase and after is, in my view, primarily metaphysical rather than psychological, although his preoccupation with aesthetic responses clearly produces an interface with psychology. In his discussion of *Über naive und sentimentalische Dichtung* Kühnemann's comments suggest lines of inquiry without fully working them out. He breaks with the predominant trend of taking Goethe as starting point; rather, he relates Schiller's categories of *naive* and *sentimental* to his interest in the beautiful and the sublime. He then raises some of the issues connected with Schiller's shifting terminology — the definition of the word *nature*, for example — and the inconsistencies in his argument, while emphasizing Schiller's exploration of the practical problems of the poet in the modern world.

Karl Vorländer's Schiller essays of 1894 and 1898 are more typical of the Neo-Kantian approach, which was to show Schiller's aesthetics as extending and supplementing Kant. They benefited greatly from the publication between 1892 and 1896 of the first complete edition of Schiller's letters, edited by Fritz Jonas. This edition allowed a clearer view of Schiller's contacts with a host of acquaintances in Weimar, Jena, and Stuttgart and thus led to a better appreciation of the range and development of his ideas. The essays, revised and republished in 1907 as three chapters of *Kant — Goethe — Schiller*, combine a scholarly approach with an accessible style. The first chapter is a thorough account of the historical progression of Schiller's relationship to Kant, taking the story beyond the years of his main philosophical activity via the philosophical poetry. The detail in this essay makes it a useful foundation for the examination of Schiller's works and the ideas in them. The philosophical implications of the difference in Kant's and Schiller's views are treated in the two following chapters, which explore Schiller's attempted synthesis of the moral and the aesthetic in his concepts of the beautiful and the sublime. Vorländer wishes to challenge the prevalent view that Schiller condemned Kant's moral rigorism and attempted in *Über Anmut und Würde* to mitigate it. He says that Schiller never challenged Kant's transcendental method and the strict separation of the realm of nature from the realm of reason, yet Schiller did feel that Kant's analysis of practical reason did not allow him to take account of the fact that human beings experience life as an integrated whole and bring an integrated consciousness to that experience. Human feeling has to be accommodated, and it is human feeling in the aesthetic response that allows the possibility of moral grace as exhibited by the schöne Seele, a contradiction in terms in Kant's system but a possibility in the realm of the aesthetic through the aesthetic contemplation of moral harmony. Vorländer stresses that Schiller calls the schöne Seele "bloß eine Idee" [merely an idea] and highlights how, having set it up, Schiller himself loses confidence in it. He sees Schiller as having much more to say about the sublime, an area in which he is also more in tune with Kant. Those who see Schiller's highest achievement as the construction of the notion of the schöne Seele are therefore implicitly challenged by Vorländer, who, though he attempts to bring coherence into Schiller's thought, does not emphasize the beautiful at the expense of the sublime. However, his insistence on the separation of the aesthetic from the moral realm to explain moral grace creates a new problem when we come to the sublime, which is difficult to regard purely as an aesthetic phenomenon.

The Germanists

By comparison with the studies of Gneisse and Sommer, Karl Berger's *Die Entwicklung von Schillers Ästhetik* [The Development of Schiller's Aesthetics] (1894) is less innovative. Berger wishes to demonstrate the continuity in Schiller's development by combining biographical presentation with detailed exposition of the theoretical writings. His approach is similar to Tomaschek's, but he is also reacting against Tomaschek. While he sees Kant as a central pillar of Schiller's mature thought and the vital influence without whom Schiller could not have made a lasting contribution in aesthetics, he is concerned to bring Schiller out of Kant's shadow. He, therefore, frequently takes issue with Tomaschek, whose formalist prejudices he sees as having obscured his understanding of Schiller's advance beyond Kant toward an objective criterion of beauty. For Berger, Schiller's great breakthrough comes in the Kallias letters, which find their fulfillment in the *Ästhetische Briefe*. He picks up from Danzel the important comment that whereas Kant was primarily concerned with epistemological questions, Schiller was concerned with freedom and used and developed Kant's ideas in the light of that preoccupation. Berger is clearly interested in Schiller's ideas per se and considers the possible faults in Schiller's understanding of Kant as not fundamentally detrimental to the development of his own valid aesthetic. This approach to the question of Schiller and Kant could be a productive one, but it is combined with a selective treatment of the aesthetic writings that tends to harmonize their content and to favor certain ideas — that of the schöne Seele in particular — at the expense of others, such as the sublime. Thus Berger criticizes Hemsen's view that in *Über das Erhabene* Schiller had turned back to an earlier mode of philosophizing: Berger dates the essay before the *Ästhetische Briefe* and claims that its argument absorbs it into the *Ästhetische Briefe*. Berger's choice of the schöne Seele as Schiller's ideal seems as arbitrary as his redating of *Über das Erhabene*. The clue lies in his citing Maria Stuart and Max Piccolomini as examples in Schiller's dramas of the schöne Seele, which suggests that he sees Schiller as having been so taken with this idea that he embodied it in his later dramatic characters.

Otto Harnack's survey (1892) of the aesthetics of Weimar Classicism contains valuable insights. One is that Schiller's concern was primarily with beauty as a quality of human beings rather than with natural beauty or, more important for Schiller's arguments, with art objects. Harnack fails to exploit this insight as much as he might in his discussion of the *Ästhetische Briefe*. He again raises the question of the integration of the aesthetic and the ethical, recognizing the conflict between the *Ästhetische Briefe* and *Über das Erhabene*. His explanation is that Schiller was in thrall to Kant's ethical teaching and that, as a result, the later essays show this uncertainty about the respective status of the moral and the aesthetic. He links this issue to that of the eighteenth-century tradition of seeing the sublime and the beautiful as evoking related but distinct aesthetic responses and thus as standing side by side rather than the sublime being subsumed under the beautiful. Harnack's view is that as soon as one makes a distinction between the sublime and the beautiful and associates the former with particular effects distinct from those of the beautiful it becomes impossible to formulate a unified and clear system of aesthetics. Harnack may well be right, at least as far as classical aesthetics is concerned, but he fails to see that the formulation of such a system was the very challenge posed by theories of the sublime and that Schiller's attempt to find a synthesis of the sublime and the beautiful, however impossible such a synthesis may seem, constitutes one of the most fascinating aspects of his approach to aesthetics.

Compared with the *Ästhetische Briefe*, *Über naive und sentimentalische Dichtung* received little detailed critical attention throughout the nineteenth century. This neglect was the result of the dominance of the issue of Schiller's relation to Kant in the treatment of Schiller's aesthet-

ics, and many of those who wrote on this subject were essentially philosophers, for whom a work of poetics was of lesser interest. Thus, the
treatment of the essay in broader surveys often has a perfunctory feel;
after giving an account of the argument, commentators have little to
say beyond some general admiring comments and some frequently un-
developed assertions of the essay's penetration and influence. The constantly repeated comment of Goethe to Eckermann (quoted above,
chapter 1) led also to repetition of the idea that Schiller wrote the treatise primarily to assert himself against Goethe — not, in the end, a
fruitful way of dealing with the work. Added to these problems was the
fact that the terms *naiv* and *sentimentalisch* were so familiar that there
was almost a general assumption that the work itself was familiar and its
argument clear, or that the classical-romantic debate was of historical
interest only and so the treatise had nothing left to say to the modern
reader. A fuller and more satisfying presentation of the place of the
work in Schiller's development as a thinker was achieved by Udo Gaede
in his reliable and judicious study of the essay's origins, *Schillers Abhandlung 'Über naive und sentimentalische Dichtung'. Studien zur Entstehungsgeschichte* [Schiller's Treatise *On Naive and Sentimental Poetry.*
Studies in its Genesis] (1899). Gaede argues that Schiller's thinking on
the subject began with a simple antithesis of classical and modern.
Contact with Goethe opened up to him the idea of using the essay to
contrast different kinds of poetic consciousness, a plan that only partially coincided with the classical-modern antithesis. Gaede links the
treatise with Schiller's philosophical development by pointing out that
naive-sentimental can be seen as cognate with beautiful-sublime. Because he is more concerned with the genesis of the basic ideas of the
argument rather than with the development of the argument within the
treatise, however, that potentially fruitful idea is left unexploited. The
philosopher Bruno Bauch's essay ' "Naiv" und "Sentimentalisch" -
"Klassisch" und "Romantisch" ' (1903) gives a historical survey of the
terms, exonerating the Hegelians from Schopenhauer's charge of having blurred the distinction between "*sentimentalisch* and *romantisch*,
and illuminating in the process Schiller's own definition of the terms.

The most extensive treatment of the essay in this period, in fact the
first major study of it, was *La Poétique de Schiller* (1902) by the French
professor Victor Basch. It is indicative of the neglect of the treatise that
in his introduction Basch feels that he has to justify treating a
"secondary" work. Yet he grasps the wide-ranging nature of Schiller's
treatment of poetics, stating also in his introduction that the question
raised is that of the existence of poetry itself — indeed of art in gen-

eral — in a modern world. Basch divides his study into two sections. The first is a detailed exposition of Schiller's argument, setting the essay in the contexts of eighteenth-century poetics, other treatments of the naive, and Schiller's own work. The second half is a detailed criticism of the essay's method and arguments in the light of the aesthetics of Basch's day. Basch's anxiety not to be misunderstood as wanting merely to demolish the work gives an indication of the tenor of the second half. He criticizes Schiller's a priori method and suggests it has been rendered redundant by the historical and psychological methods (Basch was a particular admirer of the positivist critic Wilhelm Scherer). Whereas Schiller's method is based on the notion of humanity as unchanging, a more flexible poetics, less bound to rigid categories, would admit the complexity of forms and relationships in poetry. In Schiller's own age, according to Basch, Herder gives a more fruitful lead. Basch holds to a too literal interpretation of the word *nature* as used by Schiller in the treatise, particularly at the point where Schiller states that the poet will either be nature or seek it. He also seems to mistake the defining quality of sentimental poetry, seeing the sentimental poet as one who cannot bear to look on sordid reality. Thus, in spite of recognizing that Schiller is engaging with the fundamental questions of poetics, Basch does not illuminate Schiller's treatment of one of the central issues, that of the self-consciousness of the modern artist. While his critical stance brings a refreshing lack of piety to his discussion, and while he shows how Schiller's passion for antitheses often obscures his argument, the confidence of the late nineteenth century in its scientific methods distorts Basch's reading of the text.

The 1905 Centenary

The next occasion for a flood of Schiller literature was the 1905 centenary. By comparison with the extravagant tone of much of the literature produced for 1859, the 1905 publications and the celebrations themselves were much more muted and even tinged with the kind of inhibition created by the awareness that Schiller was something of a poet out of season. Much of what was produced for that year falls into the category of tributes ("Verehrung"), sometimes of an awkward and perfunctory kind, rather than serious critical engagement. It is, therefore, not surprising that among the many publications arising from that centenary a substantial number were concerned with Schiller's non-poetic production, a field of study that offered a greater chance of breaking away from the clichés attaching to discussions of his plays and poems. Among those publications the Neo-Kantian view that Schiller legitimately extended Kant's ideas was strongly represented. While such studies again gave intellectual credibility to Schiller the aesthetician, they have the limitation of proceeding from the assumption that Kant was totally right. Thus, the insights yielded for those primarily interested in the tensions in Schiller's thought tend to be reduced.

The most durable memorial to Schiller of the centenary was the production of a new critical edition of his complete works, the so-called Säkularausgabe, edited by Eduard von der Hellen with the collaboration of numerous prominent Schiller scholars, in sixteen volumes. Each group of works was prefaced by a scholarly introduction and supplemented by a compact apparatus of endnotes on the individual texts. Oskar Walzel's introduction to volumes 11 and 12, devoted to Schiller's philosophical writings, sums up the fruits of the previous half-century's scholarship in a coherent presentation of Schiller's progression as a thinker. For Walzel, Schiller's great achievement is to have continued the Renaissance tradition of engagement with the reconciliation of the classical and Christian legacies and to have found a theory of culture that links the aesthetic to the ethical with subtlety and sophistication. Walzel makes his claim more specific in presenting Schiller's thought as an attempt to reconcile the tradition of Anthony Ashley Cooper, Lord Shaftesbury, through which he was linked to the complex legacy of Neo-Platonism, and Kant's moral rigorism, the roots of which are in the Christian tradition of the war of senses and spirit. He sees Schiller as having held to Kant's moral system in spite of attempts to mitigate it in *Über Anmut und Würde*. Walzel traces the possible channels of Shaftesbury's thought as it reached Schiller at the Karlsschule, though he by no means excludes other influences, Leibniz in particular. He stresses rather the eclecticism of Schiller's early thought and goes on to trace affinities with Karl Philipp Moritz, Goethe, and Herder in the development of an organic notion of the work of art as a product that, like a natural phenomenon, seems to exist according to its own inner law. Walzel holds that the Kallias project was successful in finding an objective characteristic of beauty and that in *Über Anmut und Würde* Schiller found a way of combining Shaftesbury and Kant on the basis of the insights of Kallias. In discussing the *Ästhetische Briefe* Walzel admits that the unfinished state of the work leaves doubt about the relationship between the Aesthetic State and the State of Reason. *Über das Erhabene*, which Walzel sees as having been published in 1801 in the collected prose writings as a means of plugging the gap left by the abrupt ending of the *Ästhetische Briefe*, is not, in his view, the properly integrated discussion of "energische Schönheit" [energetic beauty] that the longer essay requires. From this summary Walzel's harmonizing strategy is clear. His account of Schiller's aesthetics skates over the problems of Schiller's inconsistencies and thus produces a falsely coherent and unified impression of the works. He praises *Über Anmut und Würde* and *Über naive und sentimentalische Dichtung* for postulating a higher reconciliation of the opposing categories in each case, without asking whether such a reconciliation is either logically or practically possible. It may be that in an edition such as the Säkularausgabe, intended to celebrate the author and aimed at the broader public as well as the specialist, Schiller's achievement could not seem to be undermined by being presented as problematic, but such a presentation detracts from the restlessness and originality of his thought.

The classic Neo-Kantian position is represented by the eminent philosopher Wilhelm Windelband in his essay "Schillers transzendentaler Idealismus" [Schiller's Transcendental Idealism] (1905). Windelband sees Schiller as having supplemented Kant with a more psychological approach appropriate to Schiller's preoccupation with art as an experience. He regards Schiller's aim as having been to produce a cultural psychology of art, with the result that for Schiller human aesthetic awareness occupied a much more prominent position than in Kant. In that Kantian philosophy assumes a similar notion of the human personality and shows a similar preoccupation with self-determination, Schiller's theory of the foundation of aesthetic awareness in the human personality is altogether consonant with Kantianism. Schiller's disagreement with Kant over the schöne Seele Windelband sees as secondary to their basic agreement.

Two doctoral dissertations arising in 1911 and 1912 from Neo-Kantian circles mark the end of this phase of preoccupation with Schiller and Kant. Bertha Mugdan (1911) attempts an investigation of the systematic connection of Schiller's epistemology, ethics, and aesthetics in relation to Kant. She supports the view that the idea of beauty as freedom in appearance was the completion of Kant's initiative in aesthetics, even though the search for an objective criterion is misplaced. She also perspicaciously notices that, while holding to Kant's fundamental tenets in epistemology, Schiller is always moving in his use of the term *freedom* towards a metaphysical sense. Willy Rosalewski (1912) also tries to harmonize Schiller and Kant, seeing Schiller's ideal of grace as a welcome and suitable extension of Kant's ideas. He is disturbed, however, by the introduction of dignity, seeing it as Schiller's uncertainty over the precedence of the moral or the aesthetic arising and undermining his system. Both studies provide lucid and defensible positions on the questions they investigate, but as far as the illumination of Schiller is concerned their approach is limited.

One of the most wide-ranging discussions of Schiller's contribution to aesthetics and philosophy springing from the centenary was Bernhard Carl Engel's *Schiller als Denker* [Schiller as Thinker] (1908), which began as a centenary lecture. Engel was moved by a belief that Schiller's seminal role in the development of the German idealist tradition had not been fully appreciated. In addition, Engel had a passionate admiration for Weimar culture, an important constituent of which was Schiller's metaphysical aesthetics. Engel strongly rejects the validity of psychological approaches to aesthetics and thus decisively turns away from the work of such scholars as Sommer and Gneisse, who had tried to bring Schiller closer to the empirical tradition. Engel's concern to place Schiller firmly in the idealist tradition makes him ignore the pre-Kantian writings and any signs of Schiller's having brought his earlier philosophy to the study of Kant. Thus the partiality of his approach is clear: Engel belongs to the tradition that sees Schiller's aesthetics as in some way an overcoming of Kant. "Freiheit in der Erscheinung" is, for him, a pioneering advance on the tentative start made by Kant and a definition that paved the way for Schelling. *Über Anmut und Würde* is unsuccessful, however, according to Engel, because Schiller misunderstood the categorical imperative. Engel's most valuable contribution is to have drawn attention once more to the metaphysical basis of the deduction of beauty in the *Ästhetische Briefe*, making thought-provoking observations on the classical, and most particularly Aristotelian, provenance of some of Schiller's terms, the dualities of Stoff and Form and Zustand and Person being the most obvious. Engel sees the *Ästhetische Briefe* as an attempt to unite Kant with Aristotle, an area of inquiry which has still to be fully explored.

An entirely different note is struck by Franz Mehring, perhaps the founder of Marxist Schiller criticism. In a centenary publication entitled *Schiller. Ein Lebensbild für deutsche Arbeiter* [Schiller: A Life Portrait for German Workers] (1905) he subjects Schiller to a consistent Marxist analysis. For him the *Ästhetische Briefe* demonstrate why the bourgeois struggle for liberation was fought on the soil of art, reality not providing the circumstances for actual political engagement. While he does not regard Schiller as reactionary — he thinks that Schiller recognized the problems of the division of labor even in a preindustrial age — he sees him as moving ever further into a world of his own speculations.

By investing Kantianism with political significance in the essay, Schiller showed awareness of the need for change, but the world of Schein in the Aesthetic State is in fact a gilded cage. Yet although the literature and philosophy of the period left the realm of practical reality, their intellectual force and human aspirations can aid the working class in its struggle.

Schiller's Aesthetics outside the German-speaking World

If Schiller's aesthetics were slow to find an audience inside Germany, where the author was a revered figure, they were, predictably, even slower to find one outside. Some of the ideas contained in *Über naive und sentimentalische Dichtung* were familiar in France and Britain (see Ashton 1980). Though Samuel Taylor Coleridge never alludes specifically to Schiller in his critical writings, there are striking coincidences of approach to certain questions. In *The Mirror and the Lamp. Romantic Theory and the Critical Tradition* Meyer H. Abrams quotes from Henry Crabb Robinson, an important mediator and popularizer of German ideas in Britain, on lyric and epic:

> These same classes, designated generally, as the *objective* and *subjective*, were called by Schiller the naive and the sentimental, and they have also been named the real and the ideal. In general, modern poets belong to the subjective class . . . The dramatic poet must unite the powers of both in an equal degree. In the plan of his drama, in the relation of the characters to each other, all in subordination to the purpose of the work, he must have the epic impartiality; but in the execution, he is lyric. (Abrams 1953, 243)

This passage suggests the currency of the terms *naive* and *sentimental* but not of their precise meaning. One of the most important mediators of things German to the English-speaking world was Thomas Carlyle, though he was not much interested in aesthetics as developed in the German idealist tradition. In *The Life of Friedrich Schiller* (1825) Carlyle acknowledges that the level of discussion of aesthetics is much higher in Germany than in Britain, but he is repelled by the language of Kantian criticism and by what he considers the almost willful obfuscation of the truth that results from it:

> Schiller's fine intellect, recognisable even in its masquerade, is ever and anon peering forth in its native form, which all may understand, which all must relish, and presenting us with passages that show like bright verdant islands in the misty sea of metaphysics. (98)

Carlyle was highly influential in creating a passing acquaintance with Schiller in younger contemporaries such as John Ruskin and Walter Pater but also in discouraging any serious engagement with his aesthetics. The notion persisted in Britain throughout the nineteenth century that Schiller was a high-minded idealist whose aesthetics suffered from the abstraction of German thought and the excesses of German Romanticism, and in the absence of translations (the first appeared in 1844) few readers had direct access to the works. The prevalent association of Schiller with Romanticism also linked him with Fichte and Schelling, as the otherwise kindly comments in James Sime's short study of 1882 indicate: "He too [like Fichte] gave the facts of existence a purely ideal interpretation" (118). An exception to this tendency is found in the anonymous translator of the Bohn's Standard Library edition of the aesthetic essays (1875). His or her wide-ranging introduction places Schiller in the tradition of idealist aesthetics from Kant to Hegel and contrasts his approach with that of Herder. Schiller's intuitive grasp of problems for which his Kantian language was not entirely adequate is commended: "He leans upon Kantian ideas, but without scholastic constraint" (Bohn, 14). Schiller is placed within a tradition that is the fulfillment of Platonic thought. The commendable zeal of this commentator lends the account an air of missionary fervor that is understandable in a climate of widespread indifference to the subject, but the sympathetic understanding of the development of German literature as well as aesthetics makes this introduction of value even today.

Goethe's stock rose in the course of the nineteenth century outside Germany as well as inside it. In Britain we can detect in some criticism a belated recapitulation of the rivalry between devotees of Goethe and Schiller, for some English critics felt that they had to belittle Schiller in favor of Goethe. George Saintsbury's extensive study of European criticism (1904) takes a condescending view of Schiller's achievements, "which some have estimated very highly" (380). Focusing mainly on *Über naive und sentimentalische Dichtung* he concludes erroneously that Schiller had not read much. More sympathetic, though still perfunctory, comments on Schiller's aesthetics can be found in Bernard Bosanquet's *History of Aesthetic* (1892), though he falls into the common error of describing Schiller primarily as a Kantian and of associating the Spieltrieb with the behavioral theory of play as developed by Herbert Spencer and influential from the 1860s onward. Bosanquet does recognize, however, the importance in aesthetic discussion of the concept of Schein and shows enthusiastic admiration for Schiller's practical skills as a critic in *Über naive und sentimentalische Dichtung*. E. F.

Carritt (1914) is even more perfunctory. Schiller "never makes up his mind whether the aesthetic activity is a preparation for or a transcending of true morality" (34) — a distortion of a real but more profound and complex problem in the *Ästhetische Briefe*. Carritt's own position, that art frees us from the passions by making them an object of contemplation, is in fact quite similar to Schiller's notion of the effect of Schein. The most serious treatment of the aesthetic essays in the United States in this period came from Emil Carl Wilm, whose work (1908 and 1910) bears the mark of Neo-Kantianism both in approach and in its taking Schiller's aesthetics seriously. Though Schiller was not interested in epistemological questions, Wilm asserts, his philosophical phase was of lasting importance in preparing him for his later dramatic and poetic work. Wilm rejects attempts to see Schiller as anticipating post-Kantian idealism. Schiller's dualism separates him firmly from Fichte, while Hegel himself wrongly interpreted Schiller's notion of the union of mind and nature as a metaphysical theory of reality rather than as an ethical ideal.

In the gradually emerging field of German studies as an academic discipline there was also little interest in Schiller's aesthetics. The standard general work on Schiller for American students at the start of the twentieth century was Calvin Thomas's *The Life and Works of Schiller* (1902), which evinces only a qualified admiration for the subject. While there are many judicious judgments on the plays, the treatment of the aesthetics suggests that Thomas felt that Schiller was wasting his time. To respond to the centenary James G. Robertson produced his study *Schiller After a Century* (1905). Robertson, whose *History of German Literature* (1902) was for many years a leading mediator of the German literary tradition to the English-speaking world, is conscious of the distortions the German cult of Schiller have produced. Whereas the Germans cannot see him objectively, Britain and France show "objective indifference" to the eminent — though in Robertson's estimation not truly great — writer. Robertson is blind to his own prejudices and to the possible distortions produced by his own condescending attitude. To his credit, he treats the aesthetic and philosophical writings seriously as an important part of Schiller's achievement. Though he admires the Kallias letters, he is clearly hostile to the a priori approach to aesthetics, which leads him to give exaggerated importance to the similarities with Shaftesbury. His overall appraisal, which talks of Schiller's "harmony-loving mind," puts his subject firmly in the museum of dead thinkers: "Schiller the philosopher . . . looks backwards rather than forwards . . . he endeavoured to reconcile the critical philosophy with the rationalism that had preceded it" (96). In the light of such a lead from the most prominent Germanists, it is small wonder that it took several decades more for Anglo-Saxon Germanists to wake up to the intrinsic interest and historical importance of the essays.

3. From 1905 to 1945

AFTER THE RUSH of publications to mark the 1905 commemoration, the period up to 1945 saw the slow rise of detailed studies of particular aspects of Schiller's aesthetic writings and an increasing number of attempts to place those aspects within the eighteenth-century tradition. The studies of this period are too scattered and diverse to suggest a continuing debate; rather they represent the varied interests of commentators from a wide range of disciplines. Certain broad trends are discernible, however, in particular the emergence of a more wide-ranging conception of Schiller's place in intellectual and literary history and the interest, typical of Geistesgeschichte, in the cast of his mind and its development as key to the aesthetic writings. (Geistesgeschichte was an approach to literary history that attempted to define the *Geist* (spirit, intellectual concerns, and ethos) of a particular epoch by stressing the total philosophical, social, and cultural environment that gave rise to a literary work. It was dominant in Germany for much of the first half of the twentieth century.) While preoccupation with the Kant question subsides, interest in Schiller's aesthetics in relation to his friendship with Goethe grows. Commentators such as Hermann A. Korff, Gottfried Baumecker and Max Kommerell, literary experts rather than philosophers, particularly illustrate this tendency. The scholarship surveyed here was interrupted by the coming to power of the National Socialists, but the impact of Nazi ideology on the Schiller studies emerging in Germany in this period is slight. On the other hand, the emigration of many prominent scholars, such as Ernst Cassirer, gave impetus to the pursuit of German studies abroad. In the world of German studies outside the German-speaking countries interest in Schiller's aesthetics was slight and sporadic, though some significant contributions were made. In the United States Arthur O. Lovejoy attempted to open eyes to the importance of *Über naive und sentimentalische Dichtung*, whereas in Germany the *Ästhetische Briefe* continued to dominate critical interest. In France Victor Basch and Robert Leroux tried to mediate the Kallias letters and the *Ästhetische Briefe*, respectively, to French readers.

General Studies and the Impact of Geistesgeschichte

The most prominent philosopher among those who attempted to present Schiller's aesthetics and philosophy within the traditions and tensions of German thought was Ernst Cassirer. In *Freiheit und Form. Studien zur deutschen Geistesgeschichte* [Freedom and Form: Studies in German Intellectual History] (1916) Cassirer looks at different manifestations in political, social, and cultural life of the tension between freedom and form. He traces Schiller's aesthetics back to his early philosophy, noting the influence of the legacy of Leibniz in the *Theosophie des Julius*, a work not usually exploited at that time as a source of Schiller's aesthetics. The mature aesthetics, which for Cassirer were Schiller's way of discovering and clarifying to himself his role as a poet, combine the legacy of Leibniz with the new insights of Kant. To Leibniz Cassirer ascribes the idea of art and nature as in some sense analogues of each other, as well as the idea of all individual manifestations of creativity reflecting the divine (or, in Schiller's terminology, ideal beauty). To Kant, he ascribes the clarification of freedom and *Selbstbestimmung* (autonomy) in Schiller's thought. Both in this section of *Freiheit und Form* and in the relevant chapter of *Idee und Gestalt. Goethe, Schiller, Hölderlin, Kleist* [Idea and Structure. Goethe, Schiller, Hölderlin, Kleist] (1924) Cassirer illuminates Schiller's relationship to Fichte. While acknowledging definite influence by Fichte on the *Ästhetische Briefe*, both in the notion of person-condition and in the idea of art as establishing the harmony of inner and outer worlds, Cassirer sees in this attempt by Schiller to find a theory of balance and harmony a concept that is essentially different from Fichte's dialectic of the "Ich" [ego] gaining mastery of the "Nicht-Ich" [non-ego]. By contrast with the Romantics in general, Schiller's conviction that constant progression and experimentation are inevitable and desirable is balanced by an equally strong conviction that harmony and proportion belong properly to the ideal of beauty. Cassirer's second book conveys in a lively way the nature of Schiller's method. Cassirer sees Schiller the dramatist in the restless movement of his ideas and in the way that he conceives of the antinomy of nature and freedom as a conflict, Stofftrieb and Formtrieb battling for dominance over the individual. Though lacking in detailed analysis, *Idee und Gestalt* heralds a period in which there was increasing awareness of the need to attend not just to the logic of Schiller's essays but also to their stylistic features, their metaphors, and their rhetoric.

In Max Kommerell's *Der Dichter als Führer in der deutschen Klassik* [The Poet as Leader in German Classicism] (1928) we find an attempt to combat the popular image of Schiller. Kommerell, a follower of Stefan George, held an ideal of the power of poetry to civilize the individual and society. Under the influence of the cult of friendship in the George circle, Kommerell presents Schiller's development in the light of his friendship with Goethe, to whom Kommerell felt more sympathetic. He sees Goethe as having helped to free Schiller from the idea that art must bear a moral message. Art should not make people good but should restore their inner harmony. Shocked by the French Revolution, Schiller realized the need to stand apart from contemporary events and used the *Ästhetische Briefe* to elevate the poet in the light of Goethe's example as one who must be foreign to his age. Only the poet is capable of restoring humanity's lost nobility. Kommerell's determination to free Schiller from his popular image as moralizer is understandable and laudable. In its place, however, goes an equally contestable and partial image of the aesthete and Goethe disciple. Kommerell's treatment of Schiller's aesthetics is anything but profound or wide-ranging, but it offers a striking example of the reinterpretation of Schiller as aestheticist, the danger of which Jung spotted and expressly tried to combat. Kommerell's later essays on Schiller's dramas ("Schiller als Gestalter des handelnden Menschen" [Schiller's Characterization of Human Beings in Action] and 'Schiller als Psychologe' [Schiller as Psychologist]) are much more perspicacious and have been deservedly influential.

One of the most monumental works of Geistesgeschichte of the inter-war years was H.A. Korff's *Geist der Goethezeit: Versuch einer ideellen Entwicklung der klassich-romantischen Literaturgeschichte* [The Spirit of the Age of Goethe: A Study of the Development of Ideas in Classical and Romantic Literary History]. Part Two, in which Schiller's aesthetics and philosophy are treated, appeared in 1927 and 1930. As the title suggests, Korff wishes to show the development of German literature between the 1770s and 1830s as a continuum during which certain preoccupations emerge, subside, and then resurface in new variations. This process mirrors the importance in the Age of Goethe of the notion of development, of life as a constant negotiation between the rational and the irrational, the mind and the senses. Accordingly, Korff sees Schiller's mature aesthetics as the fulfillment of his own early tendencies and of the tendencies of the Sturm und Drang. Kant's influence tends, thus, to be played down, and the Kallias letters, Schiller's most direct attempt to appropriate the Kantian system and adapt it for his aesthetics, are seen by Korff as an essentially private communication and not, therefore, as enjoying the status of published work. The Kallias letters and *Über Anmut und Würde* are stages of a quest to find a reconciliation or balance of these two forces of mind and senses, which Schiller, under Kant's influence, redefines as freedom and nature. The process culminates in the *Ästhetische Briefe*, where Vernunft [reason] itself becomes second nature; nature, the warcry of the Sturm und Drang, is fulfilled in the classical notion of aesthetic humanity, where reason and sense work in harmony.

In 1933 the National Socialists came to power in Germany, causing many writers and academics to emigrate. The production of literature was strictly controlled, and the universities were "gleichgeschaltet" [coordinated], in order to harness their teaching and research more effectively to National Socialist aims and to make them ineffective as a potential source of opposition. The image of Schiller employed by the regime derived from the popular nationalist tradition of the later nineteenth century, when Schiller was held to epitomize the German character and his heroic struggle to stand for the struggle of the Germans for unity. The 1934 commemoration of Schiller's birth, for example, was used by the regime to lend itself cultural legitimacy, though this elevation of Schiller reached nothing like the level of popular enthusiasm of 1859, for Schiller was no longer the object of interest he had been in the nineteenth century. Nazi ideology did affect serious Schiller scholarship, however, and some studies appeared that were strongly colored by the cultural and racial prejudices of the regime. (A useful general survey is provided by Georg Ruppelt in *Schiller im nationalsozialistischen Deutschland* [Schiller in Nazi Germany], Stuttgart: Metzler, 1981). Fortunately, such distortions did not, on the whole, find their way into specialist criticism of Schiller's aesthetics, although they did affect the presentation of his aesthetics in general treatments, which were more likely to be ideologically colored. Werner Deubel's criticism (1935), for example, is strongly influenced by Nazi thinking. He sees Schiller's engagement with Kant as a disastrous rejection of "biocentric" thinking, of a Dionysiac, Nietzschean character, in favor of a "logocentric" philosophy that took him away both from Goethe and from his vocation as a tragedian.

Two large general studies appeared in Germany in the 1930s, and they could hardly have been more different in style, in method and in their underlying assumptions. Herbert Cysarz's *Schiller* (1934) combines religious rhetoric with nationalist ideology in its presentation of Schiller's great mission of national regeneration. The *Ästhetische Briefe* are presented as central to that mission. It illustrates the tendency of the geistesgeschichtlich approach to become excessively abstract; the style of the book is bombastic and reference to actual works is nebulous, so that it is not merely unprofitable for close study but is, indeed, unreadable. By contrast, Reinhard Buchwald's two-volume *Schiller* of 1937 is a critical biography rooted in close attention to the detail of Schiller's life; and although Buchwald devotes proportionally much greater attention to his subject's early years, he gives a readable and reliable account of Schiller's main speculative phase. Schiller was drawn to Kant, Buchwald contends, by the twin forces of "freedom" and "idea" when he first approached Kant in 1791, and yet by 1794, through his own reading of Kant and his contact with Goethe, he saw where Kant needed to be modified and supplemented. Admittedly, Buchwald's approach has the limitations of the biographical approach; we have little sense of what Schiller achieved as a philosopher, for Buchwald stresses the process of clarification of Schiller's ideas as prelude to a return to poetry, and the individual works are not examined in detail. He nevertheless provides a solid and reliable biographical framework in which to read the texts.

The most fruitful and stimulating piece of writing on Schiller's aesthetics during the Third Reich was a lecture delivered by the distinguished educational theorist and philosopher Eduard Spranger to the Prussian Academy of Sciences, *Schillers Geistesart gespiegelt in seinen philosophischen Schriften und Gedichten* [Schiller's Cast of Mind Reflected in his Philosophical Writings and Poems] (1941). Spranger's aim is to penetrate to an understanding not of Schiller's personality or character but of his intellectual constitution. His starting point is the recognition of the complexity of Schiller's mind and the contradictoriness of his philosophy, enshrined as it is in "diese unsagbar schwer verständlichen Werke" [these unutterably difficult works]. Spranger's attention is not, therefore, focused on the objective logic of Schiller's arguments but on the fundamental tension in his mental makeup, which draws him now to a philosophy of harmony, now to an acceptance of conflict and the tragic, a tension Spranger sees as having existential roots. That Schiller, on balance, spends more time developing notions of harmony suggests to Spranger that even the tragic vision contains an element of the positive, the vindication of the ideal beyond the realm of human suffering and conflict. His aim, however, is not so much to prove this limited thesis as to bring to light the dynamics of Schiller's thinking and the stages of his development as a thinker. He brings out the tensions in Schiller's early philosophy between the enthusiastic assertion of the harmony of the universe (*Theosophie des Julius*) and the lack of sensuous engagement in his early poetry or in his medical dissertation on the connection between the animal and spiritual nature of human beings, in spite of his attempt there to give the body its due. The harmony that he praises in the universe is not matched, as it is in the early Goethe, by his own inner harmony. Spranger designates his early philosophy "panentheism": that is, he sees the world is an image of the divine, but he shies away from the monism of true pantheism.

The "Intervall," Spranger's term for the period between *Don Carlos* and *Wallenstein*, was a period in which Schiller had to address these inner conflicts, a period in which philosophy and aesthetics freed him for new poetic work. While the strongly dualistic Kant side of him was still in conflict with the monistic Goethe side (Spranger admits that this is an oversimplified scheme), this tension becomes fruitful in his thought and forces him to attempt the characteristic synthesis of his mature aesthetics. At the same time, Spranger makes the important observation that no single aesthetic work contains the summation of Schiller's thought; all reflect only stages where certain ideas predominate. In the Kallias letters Spranger sees Schiller's attempt, before his friendship with Goethe, to gain a more positive view of nature, nature seen with an aesthetic gaze. In *Über Anmut und Würde* we see Schiller pulled in two directions by the monistic (grace) and the dualistic (dignity) sense of life. Spranger sees the poem "Das Ideal und das Leben," however, as the correction of his objection to Kant's moral rigorism — the final harmony and reconciliation achieved by Heracles coming only after the earthly struggle is over. The final version of the *Ästhetische Briefe* is similarly the product of conflicting impulses, the Augustenburg letters placing the aesthetic at the stage that leads on to moral refinement, whereas in the later version art liberates into a third realm. Spranger skirts the question whether Schiller could actually have accommodated his notion of the sublime within his idea of the beautiful ('das Idealschöne') of the *Ästhetische Briefe*, but certainly he sees this unfinished project as an attempt at synthesis of the sublime and the beautiful that is typical of Schiller. But he warns again against taking the harmonizing position as absolute. Temptation to place the aesthetic above the moral gives way to the reverse order in the treatise *Über das Erhabene*. Spranger provides invaluable guidance through the difficulties of Schiller's shifting meanings of aesthetic and nature. He also provides a more complex and differentiated view of Schiller's intellectual relationship to Goethe.

Detailed Studies

The broad sweep of some of the general studies forms a contrast with the continuing, though relatively slow, emergence of detailed studies of individual works on specific problems. A fascinating and, up to that time, unique contribution to the appreciation of the importance of Schiller's idea of aesthetic education was made by Carl Gustav Jung in *Psychological Types* (1921). Jung says that "Friedrich Schiller seems to have been the first to attempt a conscious differentiation of typical attitudes on a large scale and to give a detailed account of their peculiarities"(1923, 67). He proceeds to a detailed discussion of the *Ästhetische Briefe* with a brief coda on *Über naive und sentimentalische Dichtung*, of which he says that the types of the realist and idealist occupy the same position in Schiller's scheme as those of the extravert and introvert, Jung's two basic types, occupy in Jung's system. Jung's approach is two-pronged. He looks at Schiller himself as an example of the introverted thinking type, while also analyzing Schiller's view of the operation of art on the psyche. Thus, while recognizing that Schiller's account springs in part from his own psychological determinants, Jung also lays great weight on the features of Schiller's theory that he sees as being of enduring validity. He views Schiller as having identified in cultural differentiation the root cause of dissociation of the basic functions of the psyche. Individual culture has not kept pace with our collective culture. The mass enslavement of the ancient world has been transferred into the individual psyche. Jung justifiably criticizes Schiller's idealization of ancient Greek society, but he rightly identifies its origin in the longing for individual culture. Where Jung misinterprets Schiller's analysis of cultural crisis is in claiming that Schiller saw the root of his century's barbarism in the fact that reason had had so little effect, whereas in fact Schiller, like Jung, sees the problem in the lack of development of the feeling person to match the new freedom of the intellect. Jung also pushes Schiller too far toward Rousseau in claiming that he yearns for a Golden Age of precivilized harmony. While the Greeks represent for Schiller a maximum of harmony between moral human being and natural environment, the early letters make clear that Schiller sees man's past as having been a struggle for power and survival. In spite of the limitations of Schiller's approach — limitations Jung views as deriving from Schiller's own type — Jung sees the notion of the *Spieltrieb* as corresponding in function to his own notion of fantasy activity, that activity that is both creative and receptive and that gives rise to the symbols that mediate between the rational and the unconscious part of the psyche. Jung interprets Schiller's theory of beauty as being essentially a theory of the symbol. To free Schiller's ideas "from the all too constricting mantle of aestheticism" (1923, 121) he links them to Eastern philosophy. For Jung, the love of beauty is lacking in moral force, a view Schiller tries to hold at bay in the *Ästhetische Briefe* and one he would no doubt have felt destroyed his whole argument. In spite of his own at times blinkered view of the eighteenth century, Jung sees Schiller as having an intuitive grasp of psychological realities. Jung's approach has to be used with care, however, for while there is an undoubted psychological element to Schiller's argument, it has a metaphysical base that Jung does not show he has grasped.

The *Ästhetische Briefe* continued to claim the greater part of any detailed critical attention. Prominent among these studies are Wilhelm Böhm's examination of the work (1927) and Hans Lutz's analysis of Schiller's complex and changing ideas of nature and culture (1928), which also devotes a large section to it. Böhm's study is mainly concerned with the system of Schiller's argument, for he believes that the lack of such studies indicates that Schiller is not taken seriously as a philosopher. He combines detailed exposition of the individual letters with wide-ranging general conclusions about the work's method and significance and about Schiller's relation to Kant and other German idealist philosophers. He also links his study to Schiller's philosophical poems. Böhm sees Schiller as having insurmountable difficulties in devising a comprehensive systematic approach to his subject matter that would encompass all the polarities he wished to accommodate: hence the change of methodological base from the middle to the later group of letters. Schiller wishes to develop a philosophy of culture that will mediate between the empirical and the metaphysical approaches. He begins with the empirical-historical context of art as a cultural phenomenon. He then moves on to the concepts of melting and energetic beauty developed on both a subjective and an objective base and finally moves to beauty as a "world principle," developed, Böhm claims, on the basis of Schiller's version of an "Identitätsphilosophie" [philosophy of identity]. While using Kantian terms, Schiller departs so much from the Kantian meaning of those terms that he can only be seen as using Kant's framework and method for his own purposes. Yet while calling him an "Identitätsphilosoph" in his theory of beauty, Böhm also stresses that he was a dualist, for whom final syntheses were not always possible or desirable. Böhm's insights are arguably more cogent in general than they are in particular. There are errors of interpretation that create some of the difficulties he sees in the work. For example, he wrongly interprets Letter Three as suggesting that Schiller actually believed in a Rousseauean state of nature as a historical reality. He confusingly argues that the aesthetic or the beautiful mean the same as culture. He does, however, identify one of the problems in interpretation of the letters: Schiller's method of proceeding by setting up a series of antitheses that are left partially unresolved, though one of the terms may be used to build a new antithesis. This method Böhm sees as part of the experimental nature of Schiller's argument and strategy.

Lutz begins his study *Schillers Anschauungen von Kultur und Natur* [Schiller's Views on Culture and Nature] by expressing concern that Schiller's central ideas on human culture have not been identified and developed further because of a piecemeal approach to the critical analysis of his aesthetic works, the three main treatises in particular. There is a gulf between the interests and methods of philosophers, who concern themselves with systematic analysis, and those of philologists, whose work has to lay the foundation for systematic examination. Lutz aims to rectify this situation by precise definition of the concept of culture in Schiller's works from the beginning of his philosophy, along with attention to the shifting meanings of the term *nature*, to which the concept of culture is inevitably related. This procedure can lead to a fragmentation of individual works and a frequent loss of focus on the main argument that are in the end confusing. Lutz manages, however, to hold the study together with pertinent general analyses. The decisive turn in Schiller's notion of nature he takes to occur in the engagement with Kant, but he sees as profoundly un-Kantian the attempt in the Kallias letters to make freedom and nature mirror one another. The most controversial part of the book by far is the section devoted to the *Ästhetische Briefe*. Unlike other commentators Lutz devotes a great deal of space to the Augustenburg letters because the transition from these letters to the *Ästhetische Briefe* forms the basis of his argument about the latter. This argument is that the lack of clarity in the work derives from the intermingling of different layers of conception. This intermingling results in a complete reversal of some of the ideas as between the earlier letters (closer to the Augustenburg originals) and the later ones, which are built on a new concept of the aesthetic. Thus, the finished work has an opaque structure. Arguments are begun and never finished (the "experimental" style of argument identified by Böhm; Böhm's and Lutz's works were written quite independently of each other), the link from one letter to the next is blurred, and the notion of education disappears altogether. The earlier stratum Lutz sees as putting forward a three-stage development in human culture from the physical via the aesthetic to the moral. The later stratum attempts a synthesis of the physical and the moral in the aesthetic. At the point where Schiller says that beauty is a gift of nature, Lutz claims, the educational goal of the treatise has been abolished. As he moved away from the first stratum, Lutz suggests, Schiller turned increasingly toward his own aesthetic deliberations and lost interest in the framework of culture, history, and politics that he had erected for the argument in the earlier letters. Lutz's view is extreme, and in spite of all his painstaking separation of the different uses of terms, he is capable of fundamental errors, such as claiming, like Böhm, that Schiller believed a state of nature in Rousseau's sense actually existed. Also, the fragmentation that results from his reading inevitably leads to the conclusion that Schiller was incompetent, in spite of the care he took with the work and the satisfaction he expressed about the coherence of the argument. Yet at the same time Lutz confronts one of the most difficult aspects of interpretation, the relation of the State of Reason to the Aesthetic State and the consequent difficulty of knowing the position aesthetic education occupies in the scheme set out in the early letters. By suggesting such a drastic discontinuity of argument Lutz takes the opposite course to critics who harmonize the works.

The organicist approach to Schiller's philosophy and aesthetics, which was the new departure offered by Robert Sommer in 1892, was taken up again in a thought-provoking but little noticed study by Franz Koch, *Schillers philosophische Schriften und Plotin* [Schiller's Philosophical Writings and Plotinus] (1926). Up to that point there had been frequent references in the critical literature to possible points of coincidence between Schiller and Plotinus and, in connection with Schiller's early philosophy, poetry and medical writings, with the Neo-Platonic tradition in general; but there had been little attempt to investigate the affinities in greater detail. Hermann Friedrich Müller had twice pointed to striking coincidences of thought and imagery between Schiller and Plotinus, first in a short essay entitled "Plotin und Schiller über die Schönheit" [Plotinus and Schiller on Beauty] (1876) and much later in "Plotinos über ästhetische Erziehung" [Plotinus on Aesthetic Education] (1915). The second article begins by highlighting Schiller's debt to Shaftesbury by reference to Oskar Walzel's introduction to volumes 11 and 12 of the Säkularausgabe. Koch similarly tries to trace the link between Schiller and Plotinus through the influence of Shaftesbury and the mediation of Professor Abel at the Karlsschule. Koch's own approach to Plotinus is to stress the organicist nature of his thought, a system appropriate to the mutable climate of late antiquity and one that, therefore, found resonance in the atmosphere of late eighteeenth-century Germany, when rationalism was being challenged by irrationalist impulses. As with Sommer, the most successful and convincing part of the study is that dealing with Schiller's early philosophy. In drawing attention to the many examples of Neo-Platonic emanation in Schiller's early work, Koch is on well-established territory. More problematic is his attempt, like Sommer, to trace the preservation of these patterns of thought in the aesthetic essays of the 1790s. He touches on many possible areas of affinity between Plotinus and Schiller but does not engage with the dynamic of Schiller's thought, lighting instead on specific ideas. He lays particular stress on Schiller's development of the notion of living form, which he interprets as an organicist idea. He suggests that the Stofftrieb and Formtrieb of the *Ästhetische Briefe* can be interpreted as a version of the Plotinian *emanatio* and *regressus*. Koch certainly points to fundamental agreements about the nature of art in the thought of Herder, Karl Philipp Moritz, Goethe, and Schiller, but his interpretation of both Plotinus and Schiller as organicists is open to question. Also, though praising Schiller's application of the critical philosophy to aesthetic questions, he tends to leave aside the nature of Kant's influence on Schiller and thus, like Sommer, to assimilate Schiller to Herder. The characteristic method and concepts by which so many critics have seen Schiller as differing from Herder and Goethe and have recognized his thought as essentially dualistic are obscured.

The complexities of the notion of the schöne Seele, glossed over by Koch, are also left untouched by Hans Schmeer in his compact study *Der Begriff der "schönen Seele" besonders bei Wieland und in der deutschen Literatur des 18. Jahrhunderts* [The Concept of the "Beautiful Soul", Especially in Wieland and in Eighteenth-Century German Literature] (1926). Schmeer's main focus is Wieland and he traces the uses of the term *schöne Seele* through Schiller's work, concluding that the scattered occurrences in his early work simply reflect fashionable usage. When he arrives at *Über Anmut und Würde* he repeats the notion of Schiller having "overcome" Kant and otherwise confines himself to exposition of the treatise. The detailed background information is useful, however.

Theodor M. Meyer's article "Der Griechentraum Schillers und seine philosophische Begründung" [Schiller's Dream of Greece and Its Philosophical Basis] (1928) is an example of the wrong question generating an inadequate answer. Meyer sees Schiller's image of Greece as being distorted by his attempt to reconcile Rousseau and Kant. Schiller's image of Greece changed in stages between "Die Götter Griechenlands" [The Gods of Greece] and *Über naive und sentimentalische Dichtung*, but every change left it still far from being accurate, and it remained a function of the argument being presented. The author identifies Schiller as a 'gotische Natur' [Gothic type], who, though he longed for harmony, felt impelled to invest every other culture with his own ideal of striving for the infinite. As this essay demonstrates, treatments of Schiller and the Greeks tend to be unsatisfactory because Schiller's natural affinity to the Greeks was so much less than Goethe's, Herder's, or Winckelmann's, and thus by comparison with them, a study of this aspect of Schiller yields little. Walter Rehm's monumental *Griechentum und Goethezeit* [Greece and the Age of Goethe] (1936), though much better informed and less prejudiced than Meyer's article, confirms this conclusion. Somehow the individual observations, though accurate, add up to less than one hoped.

Heinrich Meng's study of *Über naive und sentimentalische Dichtung* (1936) was the first extended treatment of the work since Basch's of 1902. Meng acknowledges the problems in approaching the work but vindicates Schiller's idealist approach and the central contentions of the essay in spite of the obscurities of structure and terminology. He examines the place of the work in Schiller's aesthetics while looking at the eighteenth-century context of his ideas. In the *Ästhetische Briefe*, with which Meng is concerned to establish continuity of ideas, he notes the a priori approach to beauty, the notion of the unified foundation to the human personality, and the fact that the conceptual pair naive-sentimental is cognate with the pair beautiful-sublime. The additional impetus needed to make these ideas fruitful in a new poetics came from Goethe, though Meng does not overstress the treatise as Schiller's self-assertion against Goethe. Instead, he lays more emphasis on the intellectual background of Schiller's inquiry, examining the rise of the sentimental attitude in the eighteenth century and the cultural crisis that brought forth the search for nature as an ideal. He notes also that in the context of the framework of cultural development that Schiller constructs for his argument the naive, though it inspires admiration, becomes a peripheral phenomenon, while the sentimental becomes the norm. In spite of all its problems, Meng sees Schiller's distinction as philosophically valuable as well as practically fruitful; by using the a priori method Schiller could establish the concept of poetry as the expression of full humanity, a concept under which the naive and the sentimental could be subsumed, while freeing literature from artificial and inappropriate standards of judgment. Meng recognizes the historical importance of Schiller's move from genre classification to the poetic consciousness, according him the honor of being the first critic to reflect on the problem of the artist's self-consciousness.

The central contention of Gottfried Baumecker's *Schillers Schönheitslehre* [Schiller's Doctrine of Beauty] (1937), a major part of which is devoted to the *Ästhetische Briefe*, is that the influence of Goethe on Schiller's aesthetics in that work has been neglected as the result of a too-narrow focus on Kant. In reaction against the approach of Böhm, who wished to subject the work to rigorous philosophical analysis, Baumecker sees Schiller's aesthetics as the product of a creative personality, and his philosophical concerns, such as the freedom of the will, as rooted in that personality. Schiller's struggle to achieve, against the weakness of his body, what he felt destined as a poet to achieve is a vital aspect of his aesthetics, as is his deep-rooted need to come to terms with his great contemporary, Goethe. Thus Baumecker sees Schiller's departures from Kant, specifically his attempt to reconcile nature and freedom, in the Kallias letters and in *Über Anmut und Würde* as being anticipations of his need to undergo Goethe's influence and thus achieve a deeper understanding of how sense and intellect might be harmoniously combined. He achieves this understanding in the *Ästhetische Briefe*, of which Baumecker says that the model of progress set up in the first letters, by which aesthetic education leads on to moral autonomy, is abandoned in the later letters in favor of the elevation of the aesthetic attitude to life. Baumecker's rejection of the notion of any fundamental Kantian influence on the work is a distorting factor and leads him to neglect the unresolved tensions in the work and its failure to find a place for the sublime. Nevertheless, he sees, though he does not dwell on, the uniqueness of Schiller's approach, which derives the nature of beauty from his concept of humanity and thus secures the position of art in human society. Baumecker also gives a clear survey of Schiller's relations with Karl Philipp Moritz and with Fichte.

Schiller's Aesthetics Abroad

It was not until the 1920s that the English-speaking world began to give serious and unprejudiced attention to Schiller's aesthetics, and it was the American historian of ideas Arthur O. Lovejoy who began to place Schiller in an illuminating context. The degree of ignorance and misapprehension that could prevail was demonstrated in his controversy with the classicist critic Irving Babbitt. It was sparked off by the publication of Lovejoy's now out-dated but still stimulating essay, "Schiller and the Genesis of German Romanticism" (1920), in which he sees *Über naive und sentimentalische Dichtung* as playing a significant role in the changes in Friedrich Schlegel's evaluation of ancient and modern poetry; Schiller gave Schlegel the courage to follow through his own arguments. Lovejoy's article attracted a broadside (1922) from Babbitt, who misrepresents Schiller as a primitivist in the mold of Rousseau. Babbitt's deep reservations about the moral rootlessness of Romanticism lead him to accuse Schiller of indulging an "Arcadian imagination," which, unlike the "ethical imagination," is not disciplined to any reality. He suspects Schiller's emancipation of the mind in free aesthetic play as leading to a "decadent aestheticism," an unfortunate trap Schiller fell into as a result of his desire to escape the didactic and utilitarian nature of much Enlightenment thinking on poetics and aesthetics. "Spiel" removes from art any high seriousness and gives it a purely recreational character. Herbert Spencer's behaviorist theory of play is again inappropriately brought into the discussion. In his reply, Lovejoy did not have any difficulty in refuting these accusations. The refutation, however, did not have the desired effect on Babbitt, who some ten years later, in his essay "Schiller as Aesthetic Theorist" (1932) was still leveling the same criticisms and revealing again his profound distrust of Romanticism. Schiller's concept of the Spieltrieb again unsettles him. Confusing it with the imagination, he distorts its significance in Schiller's argument and claims that Schiller is contending that anything is beautiful that is the result of free imaginative play. In other words, Babbitt does not grasp the transcendental tradition of aesthetics. That he could be so mistaken about Schiller and cling so tenaciously to his misguided viewpoint derives — apart from Babbitt's own critical prejudices and belief system — from the association outside Germany of Schiller with Romanticism. For those who are not specialists in German literature and who do not share the traditions of German literary history, including that of seeing Weimar Classicism as distinct from Romanticism, Goethe and Schiller frequently seem to have so much in common with non-German Romantics such as Wordsworth or Coleridge that what to German scholars seem like fundamental distinctions between Goethe and Schiller, on the one hand, and the Romantics, on the other, are obscured. Thus, Babbitt burdens Schiller with all the sins of a Romanticism to which, temperamentally and by conviction, Babbitt was so hostile.

Lovejoy's brief but apposite treatment of Schiller in *The Great Chain of Being* (1936) draws attention, by contrast, to the Platonist

tradition in Schiller's thought. Lovejoy isolates two important strains in
that tradition, the notion of immutable and self-contained perfection
and the creative urge, which he sees Schiller as having attempted to
synthesize in the *Ästhetische Briefe* by embodying them in the Formtrieb and the Stofftrieb respectively. The result, he feels, is confused,
but he sees Schiller as having foreseen that increasing diversification
through change would be the dominant force in modern humanity's
existence. Although the history-of-ideas approach to Schiller's thought
has led to the perpetuation outside Germany of the impression that he
was more closely allied in thought to the German Romantics than he
was, it has also — for example in the work of René Wellek and M. H.
Abrams — shed significant light on his intellectual context in the European tradition.

After 1933 a number of Germany's leading Germanists and philosophers, along with many university colleagues, left the country. One of
these emigrés was Ernst Cassirer, who in 1935 addressed the English
Goethe Society on the subject of Schiller and Shaftesbury. Oskar Walzel, though not the first commentator to point to Shaftesbury's legacy
in Schiller, had given particular prominence in the Säkularausgabe to
Shaftesbury's impact. The emphasis on Shaftesbury from then onwards
is perhaps an indication that the Schiller-Kant theme was played out for
a time. It was also a felicitous choice for an address to the English Goethe Society. Rather than concentrating on *Über Anmut und Würde*, as
one might expect, Cassirer gives more attention to the *Ästhetische
Briefe*. He traces the possible transmission of Shaftesbury's ideas in the
German philosophical tradition through Mendelssohn. Though Schiller
embraced the transcendental method, Cassirer sees him as linked
through Shaftesbury to the Platonic tradition. In the *Ästhetische Briefe*
he echoes in the pairs Formtrieb-Stofftrieb and Person-Zustand the
Platonic idea of the visible world and the world of Forms. Schiller also
echoes, through Shaftesbury, the Plotinian stress on the harmony of inner form with the material. This observation is by now a familiar one.
Less familiar is Cassirer's correction of Kant's view of Shaftesbury. In
his early works Kant had pursued a psychological-anthropological
method but had repudiated it in his great critiques, seeing Shaftesbury's
aesthetics as resting on a sensationalist base. Cassirer believes that
Schiller saw Shaftesbury more accurately, recognizing in him, rather
than the Epicurean, the Stoic, whose notion of moral grace was
based on a recognition of the fleeting nature of human life and the
need to preserve one's integrity within it. Cassirer does not, however, see Schiller as departing from Kantian principles in favor of

Shaftesbury when he pursued the notion of the harmony of the personality in the aesthetic in the *Ästhetische Briefe*, for he suggests that Kant himself acknowledged the unity of the self-conscious mind in experience, while Schiller acknowledged the strict separation of the noumenal and the phenomenal for epistemological purposes. This argument glosses over the fact that, for example in *Über Anmut und Würde*, Schiller saw the noumenal and the phenomenal coming together in the moral as well as the aesthetic sphere.

Harvard Studies and Notes in Philology and Literature was the first place of publication for Karl Viëtor's essay (1937) on the history of the idea of the sublime in Germany in the eighteenth century; the essay was revised and republished in 1952. Viëtor is mainly concerned with theories up to Kant: the reception of Longinus in the 1740s, Lessing and Mendelssohn on tragedy, the reception of Burke, and Kant's *Critique of Judgment*. He sketches the place of Schiller's theory of the sublime within the German tradition, however, tracing the link between theories of the sublime and theories of tragedy, and thus provides a helpful guide to the context of Schiller's ideas.

Perhaps the most famous book to emerge from a British Germanist in the 1930s was Eliza Butler's *The Tyranny of Greece over Germany: A Study of the Influence Exercised by Greek Art and Poetry over the Great German Writers of the Eighteenth, Nineteenth and Twentieth Centuries* (1935), the publication of which in German translation was banned by the authorities in Nazi Germany. It was an influential book, though written in a wearyingly lurid style. Though she does not discuss Schiller's aesthetic essays individually in any detail, she gives an overview of his understanding of the Greeks and his use of them in the essays. Butler sees Schiller's relation to the ancient Greeks primarily as one of rivalry, guided by the need to to reserve for himself the realm of tragedy, and so she examines the development of his dramatic theory and his criticism of the Greek notion of Fate in the light of this theory. Ernst Stahl also took up the dramatic theory in his article "The Genesis of Schiller's Theory of Tragedy" (1938), reacting against the interpretative approaches of Fricke, Gumbel, and Deubel in the early 1930s, which consider the theory unimportant for understanding the later dramas. Stahl sees Schiller's theory as a significant expression of his attitude to life. The moral emphasis in his early drama and in his comments on his own early work is maintained in the dramatic theory of the 1790s, in spite of his move away from Lessing, and manifested in the development of his notion of the sublime on the basis of Kant's *Critique of Judgment*. Stahl's later monograph *Friedrich Schiller's Drama*.

Theory and Practice (1953) gave him further scope for discussing the — for him — central importance of the dramatic theory.

The French Germanist Victor Basch, who had produced in 1902 such an unsympathetic account of *Über naive und sentimentalische Dichtung*, returned to Schiller's aesthetics with a short article on the Kallias letters in 1934. The letters were virtually unknown in France at the time, as they were embedded in a correspondence not available in French translation. It is a pity for the modern reader that Basch therefore feels obliged to devote so much space to exposition of the content of the letters — though the clarity of that exposition makes it a useful aid to study — because his summing-up contains several striking critical comments that the reader would gladly see pursued in more detail. Basch sees the Kallias letters as the most important source of Schiller's aesthetics and regrets that the *Ästhetische Briefe* continue to receive the lion's share of the attention. He sees Schiller in the Kallias letters as having developed Kant in a Kantian sense. He notes that Kant himself, while insisting on the subjective nature of aesthetic judgments, comes close in the *Critique of Judgment* to suggesting that beautiful objects, by the nature of the uniform and universal response they occasion, do have objective characteristics, even though his system cannot allow him to make this claim. Schiller also develops Kant's idea of the beautiful as symbol of the moral by making an original and explicit link between beauty and practical reason. Basch notes that, unlike Kant's, Schiller's main focus is the beautiful in human beings rather than in art objects. Basch overstates the extent to which the *Ästhetische Briefe* break with the Kallias letters and represent a return to Schiller's earlier idea of art as mediation between mind and senses.

In 1943 a German-French edition of the *Ästhetische Briefe, Lettres sur l'Education Esthétique de l'Homme*, translated and edited by the eminent French Germanist Robert Leroux, was published. This edition developed from an article by Leroux published in 1937: "Schiller, théoricien de l'état." This essay is remarkable in that once more it brings into the discussion the political aspects of the *Ästhetische Briefe*, which had almost dropped from view entirely since the later part of the nineteenth century. Focusing almost exclusively on the *Ästhetische Briefe* Leroux claims that Schiller's goal is the Vernunftstaat [State of Reason], which will be brought about by the creation of aesthetic human beings. While the early part of this article tends to flatten out the problems of reconciling the beginning and ending of the treatise, Leroux does highlight some important aspects. He draws attention, for example, to the possible utopian element in Schiller's vision, to the logical conclusion of the process described in the work whereby the state will wither away and only civil society will be left (an interpretation often advanced or discussed subsequently by Marxist critics). Leroux's dense and wide-ranging introduction to his edition of the *Ästhetische Briefe* is particularly strong on the intellectual background of the work. He looks at Schiller's aesthetic ideas before and after the encounter with Kant, bringing out lucidly Kant's approach to the question of aesthetic judgment and Schiller's adaptation of his ideas. He gives compact but precise accounts of the Kallias letters and of *Über Anmut und Würde*. He also explores Schiller's political views and the development of his philosophy of history up to the *Ästhetische Briefe*, giving more extensive coverage than virtually all earlier commentators (with the possible exception of Tomaschek) to Schiller's friendship with Wilhelm von Humboldt and its impact on Schiller's political thought. It is striking that after many years in which the political aspects of the work had been almost completely left to one side, the crisis in Europe should trigger new attempts to read the work as Schiller's attempt to engage with the times, "to furnish proof that his aesthetic speculations could add to the happiness of humanity" (Leroux 1943, p.5, my translation). Leroux, unfortunately, again presents the relation between the early letters and the later too simply. He solves the problem of the relation between the State of Reason and the Aesthetic State (an issue he sidesteps in the article) by declaring them to be one and the same and also ignores the possible pessimism of the ending.

The years 1943 and 1944 brought two further publications outside Germany that attempt to correct misconceptions about the theory of play in the *Ästhetische Briefe*, and though neither is a detailed study of the text, both relate it to a broader context. The first was the English educationalist Sir Herbert Read's *Education through Art* and the second was Ernst Cassirer's final contribution to Schiller scholarship in his *Essay on Man*. There is something of a parallel between the circumstances in which the *Ästhetische Briefe* and Read's work arose, for *Education through Art* came into being in the immediate aftermath of the the Allied bombing of Cologne, just as Schiller's treatise arose against the background of the Terror in France. Both writers were convinced that the solution was to help human beings relate action to feeling. Read sees Schiller as the only person in the modern world who has taken up Plato's thesis, in the way that Plato meant it, that art should be the basis of education. Read's main concern is how to put this thesis into practice in education. If such education succeeded, "Idealism would then no longer be an escape from reality: it would be a simple human response to reality" (12). Cassirer's *Essay on Man* is a wide-ranging discussion of human cultural endeavor in the light of the modern breakdown of consensus about humanity's place in the universe. In his chapter "Art" Cassirer surveys the theories of art, defining aesthetic experience in ways that strongly resemble Schiller's accounts and rehabilitating the idealist approach to aesthetics. Specifically, he sets right the misconception repeated in a number of Anglophone histories of aesthetics that Schiller's theory of play resembles that of Darwin, Spencer, or any other biological or sociological theory of play. In a lecture, "The Third Realm of Education" (1960), Read draws attention to Cassirer's distinction between Schiller's and other theories of play. That he writes, "Only Ernst Cassirer seems to have grasped the essential difference between Schiller's theory of play and the various biological and sociological theories" (56) indicates the extent to which Schiller's idea was misunderstood. In this lecture Read focuses on the psychological problem of the division of labor, seeing Schiller's solution as being in harmony with both the Platonic and Confucian traditions.

4. The Postwar Boom

IN COMMON WITH other fields of German literary studies, the volume of Schiller criticism has exploded since the 1950s. To give an overview and to highlight the areas of most intense research interest, I have arranged the material from 1945 to the present thematically under a series of headings. Inevitably, many books and articles could find a place under several headings, and the demarcations are not meant to be rigid. I have attempted, by cross-referencing, to alert the reader to other related criticism. To retain the sense of development, I have treated the criticism chronologically within each section.

In the aftermath of World War II the field of German literary studies in the new Federal Republic of Germany took on a careful, subdued, conservative character. Schiller's place in the humanist tradition was emphasized, and the qualities that had made him less acceptable to the Third Reich — his cosmopolitanism, his concern for human totality and moral self-determination, his belief in the centrality of art as a human activity — were brought again to the fore. This atmosphere was not conducive at the outset to the development of new approaches to Schiller criticism. In the German Democratic Republic Schiller again often served the purpose of political propaganda, and his dramas were often interpreted with emphasis on their supposed revolutionary political stance. In the criticism of his aesthetics — which was in any case not enthusiastically pursued — the tone was set by the work of the Hungarian Marxist critic Georg Lukács, who attempted to characterize the aesthetics as caught between Kant and Hegel and as suffering from the inevitable ideological inadequacies of that age. Western criticism of the 1950s and early 1960s has to be read with an awareness of the ideological tension between the two German states. From the later 1960s onwards "Ideologiekritik" — the critical examination of the underlying assumptions and value systems of an author, usually from a Marxist perspective — made its impact on Schiller criticism. The criticism of the late 1970s and 1980s reflected the boom in Enlightenment studies and the emphasis on the empirical tradition. Such broad intellectual tendencies have had a greater impact on the criticism of Schiller's aesthetics than have innovations in literary theory.

Editions and General Studies

The *Ästhetische Briefe* stand at the center of the first major general study in German of the postwar period, Melitta Gerhard's *Schiller* (1950). The author was profoundly influenced in the 1920s by Stefan George's aestheticism and his predilection for Goethe over Schiller. Thus, she presents Schiller's development as a progressive abandonment of his youthful concern for contemporary reality in the direction of attitudes that would make him ready to receive Goethe's influence. There is something in common here, and again it is attributable to George's influence, with the line of interpretation pursued by Max Kommerell in *Der Dichter als Führer in der deutschen Klassik*. For Gerhard, Schiller was divided inwardly, cut off from Goethe's feeling for nature and his grasp of the essential organic wholeness of existence. Yet although drawn to Kant, Schiller failed to understand the latter's epistemology, even if he took to heart Kant's ethics. The schöne Seele of *Über Anmut und Würde* and the harmony of the Aesthetic State represent for Gerhard the pinnacle of Schiller's striving for aesthetic ideals close to those of Goethe. The book was sharply criticized when it appeared, and it does provide an extreme example of the tendency to overemphasize the impact of Goethe's thought on Schiller and to trivialize the aesthetic writings by seeing them primarily as biographical evidence.

The immediate postwar period saw an expansion in German studies as an academic discipline at British and North American universities. This development created the need for student-orientated introductions and critical editions of individual texts. William Witte's general study *Schiller* (1949) looks once more at the relationship between Shaftesbury and Schiller, using Shaftesbury as a means of illuminating the progression of Schiller's ideas on the question of the relation between art and morality. Witte begins with Shaftesbury's influence as mediated by the Karlsschule and moves on to discuss the virtuoso and the idea of aesthetic totality. Witte nevertheless sees Kant's influence as fundamental to Schiller's mature thought, and he brings out Schiller's development of the Kantian sublime. This was a welcome balance, as the tendency to stress the harmonious Schiller and to overemphasize his affinities with Goethe is evident in Elizabeth Bohning's article "Goethe's and Schiller's Interpretation of Beauty" (1949), which omits the sublime altogether.

The two-hundredth anniversary of Schiller's birth in 1959 was marked by the publication of a monumental study by Benno von Wiese that focuses on the nexus of the political and the aesthetic in Schiller's thought. He sees Schiller's aesthetics as a continuation of his thinking on history, and this emphasis is more marked than discussion of the relationship with Kant. For Schiller the individual is the key to success in any attempt to improve the state, and he turned away from the French Revolution, convinced that a dictatorship in the name of the people was as reprehensible as the autocracy it replaced. Here we can see Wiese ruling out attempts to appropriate Schiller for the cause of popular sovereignty (as occasionally happened in the GDR). Schiller equally rejected the dictatorship of reason alone, and Wiese sees the Kallias letters and their central definition of beauty as "freedom in appearance" as an indication of Schiller's ideal of human totality, where reason and sense must be brought into a reciprocal relationship, a process more clearly explored in the *Ästhetische Briefe*. Thus, the concern to establish human totality in *Über Anmut und Würde* and in the *Ästhetische Briefe* is part of the need to lay the foundations of a new anthropology on which a state that fostered human totality could be built. Wiese sees individual works as part of a development rather than claiming any one as embodying Schiller's complete thought, for the tension in Schiller between ethical and aesthetic thought is part of the process of finding new solutions to the problem of human totality. Wiese accepts Schiller's own justifications and arguments: for example, he repeats Schiller's explanation of how grace and dignity can alternate in the same person. He also smooths away the problem of the unity of the *Ästhetische Briefe* by claiming that the aesthetic is taken up into the notion of reason itself, so that reason becomes enriched by passing through the aesthetic and incorporating it. In spite of this tendency to harmonize, Wiese presents the aesthetics within the framework of a coherent argument embracing Schiller's total oeuvre.

The bicentenary was also marked by the publication by Hanser of a new complete edition of Schiller's works in five volumes, edited by Gerhard Fricke and Herbert Göpfert. This edition, with its compact and precise notes on individual texts, is still useful. It contains the Kallias letters as a sequence and gives helpful pointers to the genesis and sources of the works. The commentators are at pains, without distorting and undermining the purpose of an edition, to stress the basis of Schiller's ethics and aesthetics in the German idealist tradition. Thus, by contrast with Oskar Walzel in the Säkularausgabe, they dismiss Shaftesbury's influence as superficial. They ignore the systematic problem of the relationship between the sublime and the beautiful by interpreting Schiller as trying to encapsulate humanity's ethical-aesthetic calling. More promisingly, they stress the fragmentary nature of the *Ästhetische*

Briefe, which omits the treatment of the sublime, criticizing as one-sided the view of some commentators that the work comprehends the essence of Schiller's thought.

In 1962 and 1963 Nationalausgabe was enlarged by the production of the two volumes of text and commentary on Schiller's philosophical and aesthetic writings, edited by Benno von Wiese assisted by Helmut Koopmann. The volumes did not include the Kallias and Augustenburg letters, which were published with Schiller's correspondence. In the case of Kallias this arrangement is regrettable, because in their discussion of *Über Anmut und Würde* the editors are obliged to comment at length on them. The volumes are an indispensable tool for the close study of the works and are designed to make it possible for readers to follow through the influences that shaped Schiller's thought from the treatises of the Karlsschule to his mature aesthetics. In accord with the practice of his Schiller monograph of 1959, Wiese brings out the points of influence and congruence with Kant but also annotates the mature essays in such a way as to make apparent the enduring influence of other thinkers, such as Mendelssohn. In view of this broad interest in the philosophical background, it is surprising that the editors then list the writings in the Table of Contents according to whether they were written before or after Schiller's study of Kant. The political perspective of Wiese's monograph is also maintained, as is his desire to relate the aesthetics to Schiller's whole work. Thus, *Über naive und sentimentalische Dichtung* is discussed with *Wallenstein* strongly in mind. For the study of the texts relating to Schiller's dramatic theory the commentary in the Nationalausgabe is the single most useful reference work. The edition is weaker — and this function can less easily be performed by an edition — in elaborating on the systematic problems of the works.

The first substantial monograph of the 1960s was Stanley S. Kerry's *Schiller's Writings on Aesthetics* (1961). Kerry proceeds from the total impression of stress and conflict at various levels of Schiller's creative thought. He interprets the evolution of Schiller's theory as being a protracted effort to reach a maximum harmony of his impulses and ideas. The five chapters, therefore, stop after the treatment of the *Ästhetische Briefe*, which Kerry takes as the point of maximum integration, thus excluding *Über naive und sentimentalische Dichtung*. The short essays, the writings on drama, and *Über das Erhabene* are also excluded. Kerry writes in reaction to the many critics who, he feels, have tried to ignore the symbiosis of poet and philosopher in Schiller, favoring one or the other in their interpretations. He sees the aesthetic essays not only as a means of personal therapy for Schiller the poet but also as evidence of an attempt to reconcile the rational level of analysis with the myth-creating activity springing from the more intuitive level of consciousness. He provides close expositions of selected works in an attempt to make this dynamic clear. Kerry wishes to demonstrate that Schiller has the tendency to move between utterances belonging to these two levels, and that it is only by attending to these transitions that the underlying coherence of Schiller's thought can be uncovered. While conscious of the importance of Kant's influence, Kerry implicitly sees these conflicts as rooted in Schiller's personality; thus, he begins his investigation with his unpublished dissertation *Philosophie der Physiologie*, in which he perceives the seeds of later philosophical problems, for harmony is there threatened by the potential conflict between spiritual ideals and the interests of the senses. With Kallias begin Schiller's systematic engagement with the problems in Kant's aesthetics and his advance to an independent theory in the notion of beauty as the form of a form. Kerry looks at the interplay of the naive vision and the abstract argument; Schiller is inside aesthetic experience but also trying to subject it to strict philosophical analysis. "Conceptual myths are generated in the vacuum between philosophical and poetic language" (36). In particular, Schiller's intuitive vision strives for organic unity, while the Kantian system imposes separation. The achievement of Kallias is in the analysis of aesthetic perception rather than in any advance on Kant in the direction of an objective principle; Kerry sees Schiller as feeling his way toward an aesthetic psychology. In discussing *Über Anmut und Würde* he refines his view of the dynamics of Schiller's thought by seeing the intuitive level of Schiller's mind as looking for a monistic solution, while the abstract rational level embraces a dualistic scheme. Kerry is no doubt right (he admires Spranger's important treatise *Schillers Geistesart*) to identify a tension between harmonizing and antagonistic tendencies, but one wonders whether the schema would be so neat if he had taken into account the writings on the sublime and thus given full weight to the treatment of dignity. When he comes to the *Ästhetische Briefe* he tends to overlook the extent to which the sublime is a necessary component of ideal beauty, even if Schiller did not manage to show how such a synthesis was actually possible. Kerry sees the monistic and dualistic impulses as reconciled in the aesthetic idea. Identifying the metaphysical nature of the argument, he sees the mythical elements as ways of assimilating metaphysical schemata to psychological contents. Thus, the Formtrieb and the Stofftrieb are "mythical agents of continuity, hovering between the transcendental world of pure schemata, and the psychological world of feeling and force" (132). For all the extreme subtlety and difficulty of Kerry's arguments — which in their particulars are often revealing and valuable — the overall scheme is perhaps too simple. Also, the reader greatly misses context and evaluation in this study. Virtually no background to the texts is given and secondary literature with a distinct bearing on the arguments, such as the essays by Henrich (1956) and Hamburger (1957), is frequently left aside.

The year 1967 saw the publication of perhaps the single most influential contribution from the world of Anglo-American German studies to the post-war criticism of Schiller's aesthetics: namely Elizabeth M. Wilkinson's and Leonard. A. Willoughby's dual-language edition of the *Ästhetische Briefe*. The volume comprises a 190-page introduction, detailed commentary on the individual Letters, a glossary of key terms, four appendices, and a full bibliography. All of this is in addition to the thorough and painstaking translation of the work itself, set on facing pages to the original. The amount of detail and the perseverance with the convolutions of the text derive from the editors' conviction that this work is the summit of Schiller's achievement and of pressing relevance to the modern world. Identifying one of the increasingly obvious post-war cultural problems as that of the gulf between art and science, the editors plead for the treatise's call for aesthetic education to be taken seriously. Schiller, in their view, saw both the problems and benefits of overspecialization and wanted to combine the best of the past with the benefits of the present. Thus, they stress that Schiller's disappointment over the course taken by the French Revolution was channeled not into idealistic dreaming but into an attempt to tackle the fundamental problem in building a more just and free order, that of giving human beings the will to do as they ought. This approach to the political dimension of the work is in tune with that of Benno von Wiese's monograph of 1959 and reflects, at least in part, a need to counteract the tendency in the GDR to insist on Schiller's flight from reality. Although they give it renewed prominence in their interpretation, however, the political dimension is not their main focus. They aim above all to show the coherence of the work and to demonstrate Schiller's argumentative strategies and characteristic rhetorical figures (Wilkinson also did this in her article "Reflections after Translating Schiller's Letters on the Aesthetic Education of Man"), for Schiller's theory of aesthetic education cannot be taken seriously if it is not coherent within itself. Thus, they vigorously reject the genetic approach taken by Hans Lutz (1928), who saw evidence of two distinct strata of argument in the work — one dating back to the Augustenburg letters — which Schiller had only imperfectly harmonized. Instead, Wilkinson and Willoughby propose that the argument of the work is circular rather than linear. Each antithesis is only partially resolved in a synthesis that leaves scope for new antitheses to arise, antitheses that partially subsume the older ones. Thus, the editors dispose of the old problem of whether the aesthetic is the goal or the means in the treatise by seeing reason itself as taken up into the aesthetic. This argumentative method, the editors suggest, is appropriate to Schiller's desire to reflect the operation of the psyche in the form of the treatise.

Seriously as the editors take Schiller's arguments about art, one of the useful correctives to earlier interpretations provided by this edition is the emphasis placed on Schiller's vision of the aesthetic as a vital part, but a part only, of the modern world. In other words, they rehabilitate him from the widespread assumption that he wanted to elevate art above the practical realm; rather, they see him as having aimed to make aesthetic education the means of enhancing all of life's activities. Two articles develop related points. In "Schiller and the Gutenberg Galaxy: A Question of Appropriate Contexts" (1964), Wilkinson demonstrates that wrong ideas about Schiller's notion of art and aesthetic education obscure his search for a means of popularizing, of building bridges between specialist discourse and the average reader, and that this search is part of his purpose in the *Ästhetische Briefe*. In a joint article, entitled " 'The Whole Man' in Schiller's Theory of Culture and Society. On the Virtue of a Plurality of Models" (1967) Wilkinson and Willoughby elaborate on what they call Schiller's theory of "indirection" — the recurrent regression to the aesthetic state of determinability as a means of restoring psychic balance. By means of this doctrine Schiller brings into a reciprocal relationship the two models of the functioning system of the human organism that he considered essential to wholeness. The model of coordination is reserved for the aesthetic mode — a state of being in which all human powers are in equilibrium and determinate action is inhibited. The model of subordination, where one force of the psyche is dominant, is the model for determinate action. These two models are linked by the "one step backwards" principle of indirection. This theory is the most elaborate and persuasive of the predominantly psychological approaches to the *Ästhetische Briefe*.

Not all scholars are convinced by the argument that the treatise presents an analogue to psychic processes, intricate and ingenious though that argument is, and even fewer have used it in their own interpretations. One objection is that it is a completely non-verifiable argument: any rogue element in the treatise, any apparent inconsistency or change of emphasis, can be explained away as reflecting psychic processes. Another, perhaps more fundamental, objection is that Schiller's argument is primarily metaphysical, in spite of its psychological ramifications, and that this blend of psychological observation and metaphysical argument is characteristic of his speculative writing as far back as the Karlsschule. This is not to say, however, that Wilkinson and Willoughby do not have some extremely apt and revealing comments to make on Schiller's Kantian borrowings in the treatise and on his preoccupations in the realm of aesthetics by contrast with those of Kant. They also produce perhaps the most persuasive account of the notion of Schein to be found in the critical literature (to be read in conjunction with Wilkinson's article of 1955).

An additional problem of this edition is that by giving such prominence to this one work, with its image of the harmonious personality, the editors create an impression of Schiller as distorted as the one against which they are reacting. Schiller's ambivalence about beauty itself, manifested most clearly in *Über das Erhabene*, and the pessimistic ending of the *Ästhetische Briefe* are neglected in favor of the moments of harmony and synthesis in his thought. The result is the misleading impression that the *Ästhetische Briefe* represent Schiller's final word on the question of art.

In 1971 a highly illuminating and influential study of Romantic literature and thought set Schiller's aesthetics in a European context. Meyer H. Abrams's *Natural Supernaturalism: Tradition and Revolution in Romantic Literature* sets out the theory that from the immediate pre-French-Revolutionary period to the 1830s there was in English and German Romantic literature an intellectual development, which was manifested also in philosophy and was causally related to the drastic social and political changes of the day. The evidence for this tendency is the abundance of parallels of subject matter and treatment springing from the preoccupation with the diagnosis of present ills and the grounds of hope of a rebirth into a renovated world where human beings will eventually find themselves at home. Abrams draws particular attention to the myths drawn from biblical and classical traditions of the relationship between Creator and Creation that appear again in this period in secularized form. While Abrams is alive to the particular traditions to which Schiller was heir — Swabian pietism, for example — and to his links with Herder and Kant, he also sees Schiller as responding and contributing to this much wider intellectual climate. Schiller's philosophy of history, the *Ästhetische Briefe* and *Über naive und sentimentalische Dichtung* are seen in the context of the revival of Christian and Neo-Platonic myths of the fortunate Fall, the circuitous journey, and the return of the Prodigal. But in a shift characteristic of Schiller and the period in which he lived the circuitous journey is transformed into a spiral ascent, where past perfection is irrevocably lost but partially recovered in a higher state. Although Abrams says little on the detail of the texts, his breadth of vision is invigorating, and his insights provide a corrective to the German tradition of criticism which — while clearly making justified distinctions — tends to separate Schiller too emphatically from the European Romantic tradition.

Anthony Savile's aim in *Aesthetic Reconstructions: The Seminal Writings of Lessing, Kant and Schiller* (1987) is to make plain to the reader unused to German idealist aesthetics the assumptions and logical method underlying the *Ästhetische Briefe*. He presupposes argumentative coherence in the treatise and examines in particular the points at which Schiller might be felt to be making arbitrary associations or leaps in the argument, the connection between beauty and living form or the activation of the Spieltrieb being two instances. While Savile has the ability to recast Schiller's formulations in ways that bring them closer to our experience of life and art and thus open them up to discussion, his approach does not take into account some of the stubborn interpretative problems (such as the relationship between the State of Reason and the Aesthetic State, which he takes to be the same thing).

In the most recent general study of Schiller in English (1991) I present the tensions observable in the aesthetic writings as part of an existential problem but also as one rooted in the philosophical traditions he inherited. Schiller was driven by an impulse to assert a harmony with the world but also by a conviction that the world is a prison from which the human spirit must escape. The tension between the sublime and the beautiful reflects the pull of these two impulses and the incompatibility of the ontological assumptions that underpin them. It finds its correlate in the dramas, and in particular in the early dramas, in which a better world, where human beings would be at home, shimmers elusively behind the world of the play. Like many commentators before me, I believe that bringing Schiller's aesthetic essays together into a system obscures the restless dynamic of his thought. Rather, they should be regarded as a sequence of struggles with a set of aesthetic problems.

The most recent edition that includes the aesthetic writings is that of the Deutscher Klassiker Verlag. The relevant volume (1992) is edited by Rolf-Peter Janz and is stronger on pointing the reader in the direction of useful material than on interpretation of the works. This edition includes not only the Kallias letters but also the Augustenburg letters. It has a useful bibliography and also gives suggestions of relevant critical essays and monographs in the notes. It also devotes space to details of sources and reception history.

The Beautiful

Schiller's theory of the beautiful has continued to fascinate commentators, and in spite of strong interest at various times in the broader social, cultural, and political aspects of his aesthetics, there has been a steady stream of new attempts to expound the logic and explore the implications of the beautiful and the related concept of Schein. Oskar Schütz's precise study *Schillers Theorie des Schönen* [Schiller's Theory of Beautiful] (1950) is not much longer than an extended essay but is lucid and wide-ranging. Schütz wishes to stress the classical legacy of Plato, Aristotle, and Plotinus in Schiller's thought, though unfortunately he does not have the space in which to develop these aspects. In the *Ästhetische Briefe* he sees Schiller as having departed finally from Kant and as having achieved an account of beauty in which the aesthetic has priority over the ethical.

The notion of Schein gave rise to a number of treatments in the 1950s; the first was Susanne K. Langer's influential and fascinating *Feeling and Form* (1953) and the second Elizabeth M. Wilkinson's article "Schiller's Concept of *Schein* in the Light of Recent Aesthetics" (1959), which is an elaboration of some of the ideas put forward in Langer's book. *Feeling and Form* is a philosophy of art written against a background of familiarity with the German Idealist tradition (it is dedicated to Ernst Cassirer). Though she does not examine the *Ästhetische Briefe* in detail, Langer makes Schiller's concept of Schein central to her basic theory. Rejecting the psychological approach, which begins with the response to art, she begins with the art object itself and asks what it is that art creates. She concurs with Schiller that it creates illusion or semblance: "Schiller was the first thinker who saw what really makes "Schein," or semblance, important for art: the fact that it liberates perception — and with it, the power of conception — from all practical purposes, and lets the mind dwell on the sheer appearance of things" (49). Illusion is not the end of art but the first step in the creation of an artistic symbol. On this basis she proceeds to look at key artistic terms — expression, creation, symbol, import, intuition, vitality, organic form — to define how art and the various arts relate to human emotional responses. She reaches the conclusion that the quality of illusion allows the artist to present us with a symbol of our felt life so that it is accessible to our powers of contemplation. The way in which this theory of art concurs with Schiller's notion of Schein is persuasively developed by Wilkinson. Both works suggest but do not directly state that in the concept of Schein Schiller found an objective quality not perhaps of the beautiful but at least of the art object.

In 1961 Edgar Lohner took up the concept of Schein and traced its afterlife in modern poetry, showing affinities between Schiller and such writers as Nietzsche and George in Germany and Mallarmé and Baudelaire in France. He sees Schiller's sensibility as tending to extremes and, thus, as similar to that of numerous later writers. In the process, inspired perhaps by Käte Hamburger's influential article "Schiller und Sartre" (1959) he stresses the existential element in Schiller's dualistic vision. He reminds us — a point often glossed over by those who dwell only on Schein as developed in the *Ästhetische Briefe* — that in works such as *Über das Erhabene* Schiller implies that beauty is a semblance that covers an abyss.

The most extensive discussion of the Kallias letters in the 1960s was John M. Ellis's compact monograph *Schiller's "Kalliasbriefe" and the Study of his Aesthetic Theory* (1969), which is primarily concerned with the logical problems Schiller encounters with the notion of beauty as "Freiheit in der Erscheinung." Ellis gives some space to analyzing which letters he feels should be considered and to the problem of deciding how Schiller structures his argument. His aim is not to decide whether Schiller was right or wrong about Kant but to examine the theory as it stands and judge it with the tools provided by modern linguistic philosophy. Ellis finds Schiller's theory wanting. The two central propositions, that freedom can be given some kind of sensuous representation and that this "Freiheit in der Erscheinung" must coincide with what we judge to be beautiful, are never proved because Schiller cannot find a way of progressing from the first to the second proposition, and his many reformulations of the central concept are evidence of his casting around for a way out of the impasse. Ellis sees this failure as the inevitable result of Schiller's mistaken search for a specific property within the beautiful object. In the light of linguistic is-ought theory it can be seen that Schiller has given the wrong framework to his argument, for the justification for assertions of aesthetic value remains, in spite of the lack of an objective property. Ellis nevertheless argues for the lasting achievement of the Kallias letters, both as showing how inadequate Kant's results were in aesthetic matters (like a number of other critics, Ellis stresses how Schiller's practical involvement as an artist made him ask more substantial questions) and in anticipating general value theory in their separation of ethics and aesthetics from theories of knowledge. Ellis's departure from the pattern of Kant-centered treatments of Kallias provides new perspectives, even if the short work he makes of both Kant and Hegel comes as something of a shock.

In 1970 Margaret C. Ives turned the spotlight on the concept of harmony, long recognized as a preoccupation of Schiller's from his earliest philosophy to his later aesthetics but often left ill-defined. *The Analogue of Harmony: Some Reflections on Schiller's Philosophical Essays* traces the history of the use of the word *harmony* in its eighteenth-century context and contends that Schiller, realizing that Shaftesbury's notion of harmony did not do justice to human complexity, extended the implications of the word in ways hitherto unique: for Schiller *Harmonie* has profound musical, aesthetic, political and social connotations. (She explores the musical connotations in an essay in *German Life and Letters* (1964)). In the early philosophy there is a simpler conception of the harmony of body and soul. In the mature philosophy of the 1790s Schiller addresses the problematic notion of the harmony of the senses and the will in the individual personality. She picks up skillfully on Schiller's clear disquiet about the moral quality of the schöne Seele, whose true moral worth has to be proved by the ability to move to the sublime, and his consequent notion of what she calls a "counterfeit harmony" produced by the inappropriate exercise of aesthetic judgment. In the end the author agrees that moments of true harmony envisaged by Schiller are few and far between. The exploration of the notion of self-deception is a particularly original and valuable part of this study.

Werner Strube (1977) focused again on the methodological problems of the Kallias letters and Schiller's failure to get beyond the proof that an object if considered beautiful can be regarded as demonstrating "Freiheit in der Erscheinung" to the proof that any beautiful object must necessarily seem to be so and must provoke that response in the observer. Strube suggests that the problem is that the assumption of the two elements (beauty and "Freiheit in der Erscheinung") is built into Schiller's argument and so Schiller cannot escape its circularity. The result is Schiller's attempt to build up his own idea of beauty into an objective principle.

In *The Philosophical Background to Friedrich Schiller's Aesthetics of Living Form* (1982) Leonard P. Wessell argues that Schiller's theory of beauty as "living form" constitutes a nodal point in eighteenth-century aesthetics. He sets out to demonstrate this thesis by a systematic survey of the philosophical bases of the main eighteenth-century schools of aesthetic thought, which he groups under the headings of "form" (beauty as perfection, reflection of divine oneness) and "life" (beauty as pleasure, experience, sympathy). Wessell conducts his argument with great precision. He moves freely between Kallias and the *Ästhetische Briefe*, but he does so because he takes the definition of beauty in Kallias ("the form of a form") to be essentially the same as "living form." Although the broader historical context is excluded from this study in favor of a strictly systematic approach, Wessell's clarity illuminates the context of Schiller's efforts.

The Sublime

Compared with the attention given to beauty, the subject of the sublime was for decades still a Cinderella and was often only obliquely treated or introduced as an afterthought. This situation was slow to change in the postwar period. A warning against readily accepting the harmonious Schiller was sounded in the bicentenary year by Claude David in his lecture to the English Goethe Society, "La Notion de Nature chez Schiller." David takes up the complex history of Schiller's use of the term *nature* in his poem "Der Spaziergang" [The Walk], in which he notes a striking antagonism between nature and culture. The *Ästhetische Briefe* he sees as a continuation of that line of thought and as Schiller's most sustained and ambitious attempt to find a reconciliation between the two. David draws attention to the influence of Kant's historical thought in his essay *Mutmaßlicher Anfang der Menschengeschichte* [Conjectural Beginning of Human History] and mentions how Schiller brings forward the ultimate reconciliation, not content to leave it to the end of history. This advancing of the reconciliation is the product of his need to construct a classical theory of harmony, and yet this need is in conflict with his basic recognition that nature is brutal and at odds with reason and culture. Thus, David sees the *Ästhetische Briefe* as unsuccessful in mediating between the two. He points to the late-published treatise *Über das Erhabene*. While it is not necessary to argue, as David does, for a composition date close to the date of first publication (1801), it is important to recognize, as he does, that *Über das Erhabene* cannot simply be regarded as a missing piece of the *Ästhetische Briefe* (even though it arguably contains the account of energetic beauty missing from that treatise) because in the later treatise beauty itself becomes a "deceptive idol," and the quest for reconciliation seems only a staging post on the way to stressing the conflict that produces the sublime. Though he pays homage to Wilkinson, David is thus writing in opposition to the harmonized reading of the *Ästhetische Briefe*.

Another complement and corrective to the Wilkinson and Willoughby approach appeared in the same year as their edition in the form of Wolfgang Düsing's published dissertation, *Schillers Idee des Erhabenen* [Schiller's Idea of the Sublime] (1967). While Düsing is concerned to clarify Schiller's theory of tragedy (as well as his dramatic practice in incorporating the sublime), he wishes to show how intimately the sublime is bound up with all of Schiller's reflections on beauty. In addition, he argues that the ethical aspect of the sublime has been overemphasized at the expense of the aesthetic aspect. The most illuminating parts of his study concern the sublime in the Kallias letters, for in discussing the letters he demonstrates that the sublime is implied in the theories Schiller puts forward there, even if it is not explicitly mentioned. While, like Kant, Schiller uses arguments and analogies from the world of nature in the Kallias letters, he moves decisively in those letters toward a notion of beauty based on the beauty of human beings. Thus, all the factors are present in the Kallias letters that lead in *Über Anmut und Würde* and the *Ästhetische Briefe* to the development of a tension between beauty and the sublime, even though in those works Schiller explicitly tries to separate them before trying to bring them together again. In the Kallias letters, however, Schiller addresses explicitly only the question of beauty. Nevertheless, he departs in the letters from the eighteenth-century tradition in developing a dynamic notion of beauty, where material is conceived as offering resistance to form; in the ensuing struggle beauty arises by the form imposed on that struggle itself (Düsing's interpretation of Schiller's claim that beauty is the form of a form). In addition, the explicit connection Schiller makes between beauty and practical reason or freedom in that sequence of letters already points to the sublime, for it is to practical reason, in Kant's as well as Schiller's later theory, that the sublime appeals. Even in *Über Anmut und Würde*, where beauty and the sublime are separated, Düsing sees in the conception of grace the element of resistance overcome, a harmonization of potentially divergent energies rather than an effortless and already given harmony. Thus the treatise provides an anticipation of the argument of the *Ästhetische Briefe*, where the Spieltrieb harmonizes the energies in tension. Though not our immediate concern here, Düsing's study provides, in his readings of the dramas in the light of the sublime, a sensitive example of how Schiller's theorizing might be carried over into dramatic practice. Where he arouses dissent is in his emphasis on the sublime as a phenomenon of art and his consequent separation of it from its ethical implications. While Düsing rightly sees the interpretational dullness that results from too much stress on ethical sublimity, he goes too far in insisting on the aesthetic nature of the sublime in Schiller. While Schiller is at pains in *Über das Pathetische* to differentiate between the aesthetically and morally sublime, *Über das Erhabene* clearly has ethical implications — as does the alignment of beauty and the sublime with freedom.

The problem of the tensions in Schiller's thought and the impossibility of finding a coherent unitary conception of human nature behind the various theoretical statements is the subject of William M. Calder's "Schiller on the Will and on the Heroic Villain," an essay also published in 1967 and, like Düsing's dissertation, providing a corrective to the emphasis Wilkinson and Willoughby had laid on the harmonious Schiller. Calder asks if we can abstract from the essays of the 1790s an exact notion of the shape that the propensities of human nature assumed in Schiller's mind, a question he sees as dependent on the nature of the human will. His conclusion from the aesthetic and dramatic essays is that Schiller "entertained in his mind two fairly precise yet incompatible patterns of human nature, each constituting a structure embracing forces in conflict, but clad in the terminology of Kant's critical writings" (51). Schiller was unable to build a bridge between the systems, and Calder suggests that it is a more fruitful approach to the essays to acknowledge this inability than to accept Schiller's own unconvincing attempts to embrace the two in his characteristically paradoxical formulations such as "energetic tranquillity" ("energische Ruhe"). One might argue that to accept this conclusion is to break off just where the real work has to be done — why did Schiller, as Düsing points out, begin with a theory of beauty that was so riven with inner tensions? Yet Calder does illuminate the fact that behind the most systematic exponent of the classical ideal of *Humanität* there is no single concept of the interaction of the will with the personality.

In 1966 a new English translation of *Über naive und sentimentalische Dichtung* and *Über das Erhabene* appeared in the Ungar series in New York. The translator and editor, Julius A. Elias, contributed the most stimulating piece of writing ever produced on the shorter treatise and found ingenious ways of linking that discussion with Schiller's analysis of poetry in the longer and better-known work. Elias speculates that the later part of *Über das Erhabene* was completed just before publication in 1801 on the grounds that it contains a new element only momentarily anticipated in the *Ästhetische Briefe* and in *Über naive und sentimentalische Dichtung*, that of the sublime of the incomprehensible. Whether or not Elias is correct in his hypothesis that the treatise was not substantially finished by the mid-1790s, he reveals the degree to which Schiller challenges the philosophical thinking of his day. In his account of the indifference of nature Schiller rejects his own earlier view of nature as corresponding in some way to the rational mind. The element of the unknowable in nature provides scope for an analogy with humanity's moral freedom, the former serving in art as a symbol of the latter. This appreciation of the unknowable in nature drives Schiller to seek the ideal: "The very fact that experience shows the indifference of nature to the rules we purport to derive from her in itself leads us no longer to expect to find the infinite in the actual and conditional, and impels us toward the ideal and absolute which we ourselves originate" (57). Thus, the treatise contains the key to Schiller's return to poetry after he had abandoned it temporarily for philosophy — only art can channel the natural gifts that give expression to the ideal. Elias goes on to see Schiller as challenging Kant's acceptance as facts of elements in life not given to experience but nevertheless necessary as regulative ideas — for example, Newtonian mechanics or the rules of mathematics. Schiller seems to imply that these ideas are true only by convention. Thus, the world may be totally chaotic or totally determined, but Schiller has found a space for freedom and idealism through and in art. Hence the importance of Schein in his thought. Schein makes the limitations of empirical fact fall away and frees the mind to give expression to the highest aspirations of which it is capable. Elias links his argument about *Über das Erhabene* to *Über naive und sentimentalische Dichtung*, crediting Schiller with the insight that people's philosophies tend to derive from an irreducible psychological disposition. The only mediating force is that of art through Schein. Thus, Elias's exposition of Schiller on the sublime reveals how deeply embedded the sublime is in his aesthetic theory, and Elias hints at the anticipations in *Über das Erhabene* of views about the sublime that were not current until the post-modernist debates of recent years, a possibility still not significantly exploited by recent critics.

The 1970s saw a small renaissance of interest in Schiller's dramatic theory and hence in the sublime as part of that theory. Klaus L. Berghahn, both in his essay 'Das Pathetischerhabene' [The Pathetic-Sublime] (1971) and in his postscript to his edition of a selection of Schiller's short essays on drama *Vom Pathetischen und Erhabenen* [On the Pathetic and the Sublime] (1970), provides a reliable overview of

Schiller's dramatic theory and the place in it of his theory of the sublime. In *Der mitleidigste Mensch ist der beste Mensch* [The Most Compassionate Person is the Best Person] (1980) Hans-Jürgen Schings places Schiller's theory of tragedy at the point where the assumptions carrying "Wirkungsästhetik" were breaking down and about to be replaced by an aesthetic of "the tragic," as in Hegel, for example. Schings is fascinated by the connection between the development of the notions of the autonomy of the individual and the autonomy of art. The function Schiller ascribes to art in developing the whole personality brings tragedy into a dynamic relationship with the notion of humanity itself, and thus the theory of the sublime in its effect on the individual is an anthropological theory. Schings sees Schiller as fundamentally linked in this notion to Lessing, even though Schiller's tragic theory bears a greater affinity to Mendelssohn's heroic admiration than to Lessing's stress on pity.

In a number of articles Jeffrey Barnouw has explored the relation of Schiller's aesthetics to the empirical Enlightenment tradition. In "The Morality of the Sublime: Kant and Schiller" (1980) he traces an affinity between Schiller and the work of John Dennis, whose writings show ambivalence in the concept of the sublime, which is credited with creating both a harmony of sense and reason and also a disharmony, by bringing an overriding passion to bear on a conflict of feelings. On the question of the sublime, rather than following Kant, Schiller seeks to undermine and obviate the critical philosophy by showing the mutual interdependence of the faculties, whereas Kant's system depends on their being discriminated. Thus, Kant treats the sublime as being in opposition to beauty, while Schiller tries to treat it as continuous with beauty. For Kant the response to the beautiful must be subordinated to the sublime, which is linked to the intelligible and to reason. Schiller rejects Kant's intolerance to nature and sees that the latter's conception of the moral base of the human personality must be made comprehensible in terms of humanity's empirical as well as its rational nature. Thus, Schiller "takes Kant's terms as givens and proceeds analytically to redefine them by undermining their constitutive opposition." By doing so his purpose is 'to move the Kantian dualism in the direction of integration and undermine its fixed and exclusive character without overriding the tension which the dualism generates' (1980, 510). Barnouw sees the sublime as superseded by the *Ästhetische Briefe*, where the aesthetic condition achieves the harmony.

In his recent article on Schiller's sublime (1990) Rolf-Peter Janz tries, though not altogether successfully, to link Schiller with aspects of the postmodernist debate. He stresses the element of the unrepresentable in Schiller's concept, which he sees as a possible anticipation of Adorno. He also examines, but without drawing firm conclusions, the extent to which Schiller's theory glorifies violence or contains a critique of violence, suggesting that the attempt to synthesize the sublime and the beautiful might be viewed as a recognition of the need to reduce the violence in the sublime.

Schiller, Kant and Other Philosophers

The question of Schiller's relation to Kant provoked two compact but highly illuminating discussions in the 1950s, from the moral philosopher Hans Reiner and from the systematic philosopher Dieter Henrich. Both writers use the impact of Kant on Schiller and the difficulties Schiller encountered in adapting Kantianism for his own purposes to challenge the adequacy of Kant's system — something of a reversal of the days when philosophers dismissed Schiller as having misunderstood Kant. Hans Reiner devotes the long opening section of his book on Kant's ethics *Pflicht und Neigung* (1951; translated as *Duty and Inclination*, 1983) to a discussion of Schiller's challenge to Kant's ethical views in *Über Anmut und Würde*. Although Kant and Schiller seem to have settled their differences over the possibility of inclination playing some part in moral action (Reiner quotes at length Kant's reply in *Religion within the Bounds of Reason Alone*), and to have been happy to regard themselves as in agreement on all important points, Reiner demonstrates convincingly that this is not the case. While Kant is willing to allow accidental coincidences of inclination and the will to moral action, though still keeping reason and sensibility fundamentally separated, Schiller, while acknowledging the origin of moral action in reason, envisages the inclusion of inclination in morality and sees this inclusion as a moral duty. Reiner criticizes Kühnemann and Vorländer for suggesting that this reconciliation occurs only in the aesthetic realm rather than in the realm of actual moral obligation. This process of reconciliation is taken even further in the *Ästhetische Briefe*, where Schiller abandons this principle of separation in Kantian ethics. Reiner proceeds to claim the need to examine Kant's ethics and their absolute exclusion of humanity's sensuous nature.

Dieter Henrich's article of 1957 "Der Begriff der Schönheit in Schillers Ästhetik" [The Concept of Beauty in Schiller's Aesthetics] was based on his inaugural lecture. It is an indication of the article's influ-

ence and power to illuminate problems in Kant as well as in Schiller
that it was translated into English for a collection of essays on Kant's
aesthetics published in 1982. Henrich believes that the key to interpreting Schiller's aesthetics lies less in tracing ideas through the various
writings than in penetrating into the movement of his thought. While
Schiller saw Kant as having been the first to note and formulate pre-
cisely the problem of the beautiful, his own interest in the problem and
his starting point were different from Kant's. Schiller was not interested
in epistemology but in the problem of the duality of the rational and
the sensuous in human nature. The justification of art lay for him in
whether it had any bearing on this problem. Henrich interprets
Schiller's formulation of beauty as "Freiheit in der Erscheinung" as
follows: "In beautiful form and in the work of art the ground of our
moral being, which otherwise discloses itself only to the reflective understanding, is supposed to confront us in intuitive form" (1982, 244).
This formulation is the fruit of Schiller's linking beauty not with cognitive reason (Verstand) but with practical reason (Vernunft). Thus,
Schiller's aesthetics elevate the human significance of the beautiful to an
extraordinary degree and provide a test as to how far aesthetics and morality can be linked within a Kantian framework, for he seeks to explain
how the objectification of the subjective play of imagination can occur
in aesthetic experience but does not see that he cannot do so within the
Kantian system without subjecting the system itself to a critique — a
task beyond his powers. Thus, he introduces terms and concepts from
his own pre-Kantian writings to try to account for this phenomenon
and seems thereby to involve himself in insoluble contradictions. In
particular, Schiller cannot solve the problem that in Kant's system — in
spite of Kant's own hint of an analogy between the good and the
beautiful — moral freedom, the freedom of the will as expressed in the
notion of the categorical imperative, cannot be symbolized by the
beautiful, for moral freedom resists sensibility while the beautiful requires harmony. Thus, Henrich highlights the logical discontinuity of
Über Anmut und Würde, where Schiller hovers between the beautiful
and the sublime, trying to bring them into a logically coherent relationship, when in fact the beautiful objectifies in intuitive form the harmony
of the will, whereas the sublime objectifies the opposition of the will to
sensibility. For Kant scholars Schiller thus provides the demonstration
of a problem inherent in the relationship between Kantian ethics and
aesthetics, while pointing the way forward to Schelling and Hegel and
their attempts at reconciliation upon a different philosophical foundation.

In 1956 Käte Hamburger produced the first of two provocative and influential articles on Schiller's aesthetics and philosophy. "Schillers Fragment 'Der Menschenfeind' und die Idee der Kalokagathie" [Schiller's Fragment 'The Misanthropist' and the Idea of Kalokagathia] is related to Henrich's article in highlighting problems and discontinuities in Schiller's arguments. She focuses, however, less specifically on Schiller's appropriation of the Kantian system and more on what she sees as a misguided attempt on Schiller's part to interpret art and life according to common categories, in other words to find the points where the moral and the aesthetic coincide. The key texts in the examination of this problem are the fragment "Der Menschenfeind" and *Über Anmut und Würde*. In attempting to account for Schiller's failure to finish the play, she notes the change in presentation of the central character, Hutten, and attributes it to Schiller's reading of Shaftesbury's *The Moralists*. Hamburger, however, sees the crucial factor in his decision to abandon the plan as being the problem of presenting Hutten's daughter Angelika, an idealized figure whose moral and physical beauty anticipate the characteristics of the schöne Seele as expounded in *Über Anmut und Würde*. Schiller breaks off the attempt to embody such a concept dramatically but continues to pursue it in the aesthetic writings of the early 1790s. Hamburger sees the influence of Winckelmann and the overwhelming status accorded the Greek ideal as interpreted by him as making beauty the key moral as well as aesthetic concept, but she insists that Schiller could never develop a clear aesthetic argument while maintaining a coincidence between the two. His attempt to bring Winckelmann-Shaftesbury and Kant together creates a constant confusion of metaphorical description and constitutive analysis. Thus, Schiller's arguments lead always to an aporia, as the example of *Über Anmut und Würde* indicates. The notion of dignity logically excludes grace, which Schiller, having only just constructed his argument, admits is "merely an idea," and he loses faith in it for having its roots in the sensible world. Hamburger certainly draws attention to real conceptual shifts in Schiller's argument and provides a salutary challenge to, for example, the introduction to volume 11 of the Säkularausgabe, where Walzel suggests that the legacy of Shaftesbury could be combined unproblematically with Kant. On the other hand, it is not ultimately productive to suggest that Schiller's main concern in his aesthetics, namely to demonstrate that art is fundamental to what it means to be human, was somehow illconceived from the start, for not only in the late eighteenth century have people been inclined to believe that art and ethics must be linked in some fundamental way.

Ronald D. Miller's study *Schiller and the Ideal of Freedom: A Study of Schiller's Philosophical Works with Chapters on Kant* was first published in 1959 in a limited edition. It became more generally available and was more widely discussed when it was republished in 1970 by Oxford University Press. Miller convincingly claims that the primacy of the ideal of freedom is behind Schiller's adoption and adaptation of aspects of Kant's philosophy for his own aesthetic system. He discusses Kant's conception of moral freedom, followed by an analysis of Schiller's theory of tragedy, a clear and detailed account of which was valuable at a time when the topic was not fashionable. This arrangement of the material suggests that in his theory of tragedy Schiller came closest to Kant's notion of moral freedom. Subsequently Miller explores the problem for Schiller of the rigidity of Kant's conception of the moral law and Schiller's attempts to "appeal to a wider conception of nature, in which reason itself is embraced" (106) in his examination of the alternation of moral and aesthetic freedom in *Über Anmut und Würde* and the *Ästhetische Briefe*. What is extraordinary about this book is that while there is the occasional general reference to critical opinion there is not a single footnote, there is no bibliography, and no critical work or commentator is named. This deficiency reduces its scope considerably.

In another influential article, Käte Hamburger explored Schiller's philosophy in relation to existentialism. "Schiller und Sartre" (1959), in spite of the title, also involves discussion of Heidegger and fleetingly of Husserl. Hamburger is responding to attempts in the 1950s, mainly in connection with Schiller's dramas, to stress his counter-idealist tendencies. Focusing on his famous comparison of the realist and the idealist in *Über naive und sentimentalische Dichtung*, she concludes that the idealist is condemned and the realist finally vindicated on the basis not of their beliefs but of their actions, the realist acting more worthily than his philosophy would lead one to expect. This conclusion leads her to what she sees as a fundamental difference between Kant and Schiller in their conception of freedom and the exercise of the will. Whereas for Kant freedom consists in the performance of the moral law and there is no exercise of freedom that is not the exercise of the pure good will, Schiller, in particular in his writings on tragedy, separates the good will and the free will such that the will becomes the primary phenomenon and the performance of moral duty may or may not follow. Here Hamburger builds the bridge to Sartre, claiming that he states directly what Schiller states only indirectly and in circumscribed terms as part of the aesthetic judgment of tragedy.

Hans Jaeger's "Schillers Philosophie der Existenz" [Schiller's Philosophy of Existence] (1959) also stresses the differences between Kant and Schiller and draws on the Ästhetische Briefe above all to argue that Schiller's concern for human totality, for the individual potential for self-realization, underlies his concern for the nature of beauty. That realistic grasp of human potentialities but also of human imperfections makes tolerance and justice, and the individual's relation with the wider world, fundamental to Schiller's portrayal of the human condition. Jaeger sees in the analysis of the human being under the two categories "person" and "condition" the root of Schiller's philosophy of human existence. The human being as condition is linked to time, as person to freedom. In the aesthetic state (Zustand) this opposition is temporarily overcome, and this is the true state of human freedom, a freedom quite distinct from the Kantian freedom, which is based on the exercise of the moral will, as Hamburger also stresses. Schiller's aesthetic freedom is the freedom, as he says in Letter 19, of humanity's mixed nature, the freedom of determinability and infinite potential. Jaeger sees the sublime and the more Kantian idea of freedom that underlies it as assimilated in all important respects to the beautiful in the Ästhetische Briefe. While not wishing to present Schiller as fully anticipating Heidegger's position, he indicates briefly where he sees the main similarities and distinctions, stressing that both saw the individual's situation as part of a human nexus as fundamental. This point leads Jaeger to a consideration of the importance of tolerance for others as the concomitant of self-discipline and how that theme can be seen as developed in Schiller's dramas, in particular.

The result of seeing Schiller's notion of freedom in this light is a greater interest in the complexities of the "realist" characters and the political realities as portrayed in his dramas; and this tendency, of which the two essays above are symptomatic, is possibly more fruitful when applied to the creative writing than when applied to the theoretical essays. Calder's article "Schiller on the Will and on the Heroic Villain" (1967) indicates how difficult it is to pin Schiller down to a consistent theory of the will, and so, as an approach to the aesthetics, it appears something of a response to a philosophical fashion. Nevertheless, a late addition to the line of argument was provided by Walter Hinderer in 1971. Hinderer sees Schiller's conception of freedom and the human personality as deeply influenced by his living at a time when a vacuum in values was beginning to open up. Thus, for Schiller the notion of the person is central — personal autonomy makes human beings human. Hinderer interprets Schiller as having an existential notion of freedom, shown by his summing up Kant's moral philosophy in the words

"Bestimme Dich aus Dir selbst" [Determine yourself on the basis of yourself]. Human potentiality is set above human reality. Hinderer thus links Schiller's concept of human personality and action both to Heidegger and to Max Scheler. Though Hinderer explored this line further in relation to Schiller's drama, it has not been developed further as an approach to the aesthetics.

Schiller's relation to Kant and Hegel was analyzed in the bicentenary year (1959) by Günter Rohrmoser in "Zum Problem der ästhetischen Versöhnung: Schiller und Hegel" [On the Problem of Aesthetic Reconciliation: Schiller and Hegel], in which he takes up and scrutinizes some of the assertions of Lukács, and of the Marxist critics influenced by him, about the degree to which Schiller was trapped within both Kantian idealism and bourgeois alienation. He gives this approach to Schiller's aesthetics credit for helping to free criticism from exclusive concentration on Kant and for encouraging a view of the works as being on a continuum leading from Kant to Hegel. Yet he clearly feels that it lacks differentiation in its exaggerated stress on the subjective nature of Schiller's solution to the problems he addressed. Hegel's own estimate of Schiller puts Schiller much closer to him, especially if one considers Schiller's discussion of aesthetics within the context of the problems of historical development. He saw human autonomy and the forces of nature as in conflict, but that there must be some possibility of reconciliation he regarded as a postulate of human nature. The famous comment by Hegel, quoted in Chapter 1, that Schiller had overcome the Kantian abstraction Rohrmoser takes to mean that Schiller had tried to carry over the subjective reconciliation achievable in the individual into the political realm and in this way to make it part of the historical process. At the same time, Rohrmoser recognizes that in seeing revolution as superfluous Schiller made himself less able to address the circumstances of his day. He is distinct from Hegel in not achieving a dialectic in his thought but remaining caught in unresolved conflicts, just as in the dramas the aesthetically harmonious individual is still trapped within a world of malign fate. Thus, Rohrmoser's challenge to some of the commonplaces of Marxist criticism ends with some concessions to the rightness of Engels's complaint about Schiller's flight from banal misery into high-flown misery.

In the 1960s the Kallias letters continued to provide a focus for consideration of Schiller's relation to Kant. Sigbert Latzel and Eva Schaper each published a highly stimulating essay on the letters in 1961 and 1964, respectively. Whereas Latzel concentrates on elucidating why Schiller chose the procedure and logical argument he did, Schaper looks again at Schiller's apparent clashes with the Kantian system and the reasons for them. Latzel begins with Kant's position with regard to aesthetics by contrast with the rationalists and the sensualists. Kant's middle position acknowledges the subjective response but also develops the idea of universal assent and thus moves in the direction of objective judgment. Schiller strove for an a priori deduction of beauty not because he disagreed with Kant's insistence that beauty does not please by means of a concept but because he (Schiller) claimed that beauty could nevertheless be deduced according to one. His method is to set up a negative analogue on the basis of reason itself, in the course of which he shows two areas of disagreement with Kant in believing that the judgment of beauty is not the same as that of any other object and in believing that in this distinct process reason and not the understanding is operational. Attributing a regulative function to reason, he thus sets up an argument by which an object that appears to possess its own practical reason must necessarily be beautiful. Where Latzel sees Schiller's argument as falling down is in the analogue relationship of the object to freedom, by means of which Schiller could still not establish an absolute definition. Aware of this problem, he moved on to a new experiment in deduction in the *Ästhetische Briefe*.

In "Friedrich Schiller: Adventures of a Kantian" Eva Schaper concentrates on the opening of the Kallias correspondence, where Schiller sets out his proposed analysis of beauty as the fourth (sensuous-objective) possibility of the various permutations of sensuous-rational and objective-subjective, and on his definition of beauty as "Freiheit in der Erscheinung." Schaper is in no doubt that Schiller misunderstands Kant at various points, and at the very least uses words such as *objective* and *subjective* in non-Kantian senses. On the synthesis, adumbrated by Kant in his *Critique of Judgment* but actually attempted by Schiller in his "Freiheit in der Erscheinung", she poses the provocative question, "An admirable *tour de force* — or a deplorable conceptual muddle?" and continues:

> Both answers are, in a way, correct. Deplorable, because this is at odds with Kant's fundamental insight into the methodological character of his principles and into the independence of ethical evaluation from assessment of fact. Admirable, however, in the careless disregard of the system, which allowed him to resurrect and old but forgotten piece of aesthetic wisdom: form is the "how" of things, and to recognize this is to become fully human. Only this could not be done within Kant's philosophy. (1964, 359–60)

She combines a devastating critique of Schiller's use of terminology
with the judgment that he was trying to reach truths beyond the capacities of the system within which he was working. Schaper specifically
addresses Käte Hamburger's objections to Schiller's method
(Hamburger 1956) of mixing logical analysis with metaphorical ex-
pressions and vindicates him on the grounds that Kant's system lacked
the elements for any definition of beauty and that the conceptual shifts
to which Hamburger objects are the only way of breaking out of the
Kantian circularity. In 1979 Schaper again demonstrated, this time
more clearly than in her earlier essay, how confusing Schiller's adoption
of Kantian terms is for a Kant specialist. In "Schiller's Kant: A Chapter
in the History of a Creative Misunderstanding" she again looks at the
problematic formulation "sensuous-objective." Yet Schaper sees
Schiller's problems as illuminating areas of difficulty for Kant scholars
and as showing by negative example what the pitfalls of Kant's terms
can be.

The most extensive study of Kallias in the 1970s came from Fritz
Heuer. Heuer wishes to rescue the Kallias project from some of its
critics. He does not regard the attempt to find an objective criterion of
beauty as unsuccessful and expounds Schiller's thought as true to the
direction established by Kant. Heuer bases his argument on the notion
of "Darstellung" [representation]; under what conditions is the sensuous representation of freedom possible? He concludes that Schiller's use
of the transcendental method leads him to broader anthropological
questions about the possibility and nature of the representation of humanity. Heuer's thesis is thus in striking contrast to the main trend of
criticism of Kallias. The anthropological interest is evident also in Wolfgang Düsing's more general article (1975) on Schiller's transformation
of Kant's aesthetic concepts into anthropological categories. He begins
by clarifying Schiller's position at a point of change in aesthetics with
the demise of mimetic theories and of ideas based on an uncomplicated
relation of art to nature and the rise of theories of art as comprehending
the whole person. For Düsing it is not the transcendental deduction
that fascinates Schiller but the anthropological implications of the interplay of subjective and objective in aesthetic experience. Düsing traces
this concern from Schiller's earliest philosophy, devoting some space to
his anthropology of the sublime as well as that of the beautiful. At the
point when Düsing was writing the intense interest in anthropology in
the eighteenth century had not yet begun, and his essay thus anticipates
a trend of the 1980s.

Heinrich Mettler renews an old question in *Entfremdung und Revolution: Brennpunkt des Klassischen* [Alienation and Revolution: Focus of the Classical] (1977), that of the importance of Kant and Goethe for the *Ästhetische Briefe*. Mettler sees the impact of the French Revolution, which presented a radical challenge to the notion of enlightenment, as crucial to Schiller's reception of Kant's thought. His engagement with the reasons for the crisis of the age in the *Ästhetische Briefe* is also a continuation of the debate with Kant over beauty, moral behaviour and genius. Yet they also represent the effects of Schiller's encounter with Goethe's genius, an encounter that brought him psychological renewal and the ability to combine the insights of Kant's political thought in the wake of events in France with the notion of *Humanität* as a set of inward values. Mettler overemphasizes the anticipations of Kant in Schiller's pre-Kantian works. Nevertheless, he probes convincingly with detailed reference to Kant's works the concepts common to both men and Schiller's transformation of them into the program for Weimar Classicism.

The most provocative recent contribution on the Kant and Schiller question came from Paul de Man in an as yet unpublished lecture, "Kant and Schiller," reported by Marc Redfield (1990). Earlier, in *The Rhetoric of Romanticism* (1984) de Man had seen in Schiller an oversimplification of Kant, which transformed Schiller's insights into an overtly political aesthetic ideology:

> The Schiller text . . . condenses the complex ideology of the aesthetic in a suggestive concatenation of concepts that achieve the commonplace, not by their banality but by the genuine universality of their stated aspirations. The aesthetic, as is clear from Schiller's formulation, is primarily a social and political model, ethically grounded in an assumedly Kantian notion of freedom.(264)

Taking up the claims of Wilkinson and Willoughby in their edition that Schiller's text demonstrates the tautology of art, de Man asserts that tautology "functions as a restrictive coercion that allows only for the reproduction of its own system" (265). There is a conflict between this function and art's claim to define humanity in its broadest sense. The smooth surface of aesthetic education conceals the violence that is implicit in it. The harmonious image of the dance, to which Wilkinson and Willoughby draw attention to illustrate their argument, is for de Man analogous to the violent imposition of tropes upon the text. De Man continues more drastically, according to Marc Redfield's account of the unpublished lecture, in which he suggests the violence Schiller does to Kant: Schiller reverts to an empirical idealism and to a naturalization of tropological structures that abolish the ability of Kant's transcendental method to reveal the true materiality of language. Schiller understands chiasmic oppositions as "Triebe," natural phenomena, and replaces Kant's mathematical and dynamic sublime with the binary opposition of theoretical and practical. The lack of necessity in the reciprocal action of the drives is explained by reference to the human, that is, the natural or phenomenal. By chiasmic inversion the valorization of the empirical becomes a valorization of the spiritual. The aesthetic is thus domesticated and granted exemplary status. Thus, Joseph Goebbels's vulgarization of Schiller in his novel *Michael: Ein deutsches Schicksal in Tagebuchblättern* (1929), in which he elaborates the notion of the statesman-artist in a fascist direction, is a repetition of Schiller's own vulgarization of Kant. Goebbels, though distorting Schiller's text for his own purposes, nevertheless exposes the violence beneath the humanistic gesture of the treatise. Redfield, whose own analysis is also an analysis of de Man's difficulties with aspects of his own system, allegorized in the Kant-Schiller issue, illustrates the move by Schiller away from Kant with reference to the significance of the Juno Ludovisi in the *Ästhetische Briefe*. Many will find de Man strong meat, and, even if one accepts his premises, the tone of accusation, the implied ideological interrogation, may seem misplaced. Terry Eagleton (1990, see "Marxist Approaches" below) analyzes the ideology of the aesthetic, this time in sophisticated Marxist terms.

In 1992 Frank-Peter Hansen, in "Die Rezeption von Kants *Kritik der Urteilskraft* in Schillers Briefen *Über die ästhetische Erziehung des Menschen*" [The Reception of Kant's *Critique of Judgment* in Schiller's Letters *On the Aesthetic Education of Man*], insisted again on the closeness of Schiller to Kant, a closeness that he sees as particularly marked in the *Ästhetische Briefe*, more so than in the earlier Kallias or in *Über Anmut und Würde*. Hansen sees the increased closeness as deriving from the distinction Schiller makes in the later treatise between aesthetic and moral freedom, whereas the uncertain boundaries between the two in the earlier works had caused Schiller to be at odds with Kant on the question of moral freedom. Hansen also sees Kant's theory of play in his *Critique of Judgment* as an anticipation of Schiller's conception of play as representative of the totality of the aesthetic character.

Schiller's relationship with Fichte has provoked only very limited interest since 1945. The two poles of the argument are represented by Jeffrey Barnouw and Hans-Georg Pott. Barnouw, in " 'Der Trieb, bestimmt zu werden.' Herder, Schiller und Schelling als Antwort auf

Fichte" [The Impulse to be Determined: Herder, Schiller and Schelling as Responses to Fichte] (1972), sees Schiller's standpoint as much more experientially based than Fichte's. Barnouw claims that going beyond both Kant and Fichte, Schiller in his theory of beauty opened up reason to the claims of instinct, experience, and the senses in general. Stofftrieb and Formtrieb are mutually dependent. This thesis takes Schiller in the direction of an aesthetics of spontaneity that anticipates the Romantics. Hans-Georg Pott, by contrast, in his monograph *Die schöne Freiheit: Eine Interpretation zu Schillers Schrift "Über die ästhetische Erziehung des Menschen"* [Beautiful Freedom: An Interpretation of Schiller's Work "On the Aesthetic Education of Man"] (1980), sees the *Ästhetische Briefe* as the aesthetic treatise Fichte never wrote, not in the sense that Schiller reproduces Fichte's ideas exactly but in the sense that the work is in the spirit of Fichte's elaboration of Kant. The obscurity of Pott's style and the fact that he presupposes the philosophical background but draws little on Schiller scholarship makes his treatment inaccessible to all but the most determined.

The extent of the Kantian influence has been questioned recently by David Pugh, whose article "Schiller as Platonist" (1991) marks a fruitful return to an old question. Many critics have remarked on Schiller's debt to the Platonic tradition, stressing in particular the transmission of Platonic and Neo-Platonic thought via Leibniz at the Karlschule. The affinities between Schiller and Shaftesbury have also been discussed (for example by Walzel, Cassirer, and Witte). Pugh, however, unlike Walzel, looks to the influence of the Platonic tradition not to underpin the harmonious Schiller but as a means of explaining the tensions and apparent contradictions in his thought. Walzel had associated the influence of Shaftesbury with harmony and that of Kant with conflict. Pugh sees these tensions as inherent in the Platonic tradition itself. Plato's theory of Ideas led him at times to a positive, at times to a negative evaluation of the material world, and this ambivalence manifests itself in a characteristic ambivalence in the Platonic tradition with regard to art and beauty. On the one hand, the work of art is inferior to the Idea it represents; but on the other hand, art adds the dimension of ideal form to the raw material of reality and thus raises it above the material world. Though it is impossible to show that Schiller knew Plotinus, and his acquaintance with Plato cannot be more than hazily inferred, Pugh argues that Schiller shares this basic tension in Platonic thought and that this tension accounts for his wavering between models of harmony, in which beauty brings sense and reason into equilibrium (as in the *Ästhetische Briefe*), and of conflict, in which he gives precedence to reason

over the world of the senses (as in *Über das Erhabene*). The provenance
of Schiller's use of the notions of the intelligible and nature Pugh sees
as rooted in Platonic ontology rather than in Kantian thought. Beauty
and sublimity refer to an all-embracing structure of being and thus are
incompatible in a way that they are not in Burke or Kant. Schiller's
models of harmony and conflict are mutually exclusive in spite of all
Schiller's efforts, for example in *Über Anmut und Würde* and the *Ästhetische Briefe*, to unify them. Pugh insists on the essentially metaphysical nature of Schiller's categories and thinking and therefore is at the
opposite pole to those (for example, Wilkinson and Willoughby 1967
and Barnouw 1982) who see Schiller as concerned with psychological
or empirical phenomena. He also differs fundamentally from Koch
(1926), whose organicist interpretation of the affinities between Schiller
and Plotinus had assimilated Schiller to Herder and Goethe. Pugh's
perspective on Schiller's philosophical inheritance necessarily makes him
see Kant's influence as less fundamental than would many critics. Kant
provided Schiller with the most up-to-date philosophical system by
means of which to analyze problems in aesthetics, though the problems
and Schiller's characteristically contradictory approach to them predated the study of Kant. That perspective also makes Pugh insist that
Schiller's notion of harmony was possible for him only in an ideal
realm. Far from being a realizable possibility or even a utopian vision
that works upon the present, Pugh sees the Aesthetic State as possible
only in the realm of Schein and therefore as essentially illusory — as an
elaborate culture of courtesy and ornament on no account to be introduced into the real world.

Marxist Approaches

As one would expect, it was primarily from the German Democratic
Republic that Marxist approaches emerged in the immediate postwar
period. Schiller's aesthetics were never a subject of lively debate in the
GDR, however, nor was every piece of criticism, as Joachim Müller's
work (1959; see also Bock 1958) shows, strongly ideologically colored.
In the bicentenary year of 1959 Siegfried Seidel could remark that the
aesthetics had yet to be analyzed thoroughly from a Marxist perspective
(150). That time never really came. The spotlight fell more strongly on
Schiller in the 1950s than subsequently, as a result of the debate on the
cultural "Erbe" (heritage), but it fell more on his plays than on the
aesthetics. As the new state established its cultural policy in its early

years, the debates of the 1920s and 1930s among communist writers in
Germany and the Soviet Union with regard to the appropriation or rejection of the literary heritage was revived. Under the influence of figures such as Johannes R. Becher and Alexander Abusch a conservative
policy prevailed, according to which the GDR was to be shown as the
true heir to the German classical heritage. In the case of Schiller this
policy manifested itself in a strong emphasis on the social criticism in
the early dramas, on the realist elements in his work, and on the relationship of hero and people in plays such as *Wilhelm Tell*. Because
Kant's "subjective idealism" was strongly out of favor in the 1950s and
1960s, the aesthetics seemed an unprofitable field of study, except insofar as Schiller could be shown to have moved away from Kant toward a
new realism. The most weighty and influential criticism of his aesthetics
came from Georg Lukács, whose two essays set the tone for other critics. Lukács's approach to the question of the cultural heritage was more
subtle and questioning than than of the cultural establishment, while in
the West the essays were regarded as radical and provocative, as the
various dissenting voices indicate.

In "Zur Ästhetik Schillers" (1954) Lukács attempts to show the
dialectical connection between progressive and reactionary tendencies
in German idealist aesthetics. He combines this attempt with his profound concern with the nature and problems of realist writing.
Schiller's lasting contribution in aesthetics for Lukács is that in his determination to press forward with his own convictions he ignores the
problems of using the Kantian system and thus moves decisively beyond
it in a productive direction. This contribution is of value, in spite of
Schiller's inability to grasp the dialectic of history or give a conscious
critique of the idealism of Kant's system. Thus, Lukács's conclusion can
be seen as a Marxist elaboration of Hegel's own comments on Schiller.
After an early period of revolutionary fervor, Schiller, in Lukács's view,
turned away in horror from the degeneration into barbarism he saw in
Revolutionary France. His solution in the *Ästhetische Briefe* is the construction of a utopia, which in theory makes revolution superfluous, yet
one to which Schiller is unable to give stable conceptual shape because
of his inadequate grasp of the economic conditions determining his
world and because of his entanglement in the system of Kantian idealism. Though he sees clearly that humanity's ills bear some relation to
the division of labor, his analysis of those ills is much more abstract
than that of earlier Enlightenment thinkers such as the Scot Adam Ferguson. The division of mental faculties, for instance, is for Schiller itself
the product of analysis, an academic rather than a practical problem.

Lukács sees Schiller's method and solution necessarily as upside-down, for Schiller believes it possible to change people apart from changing their social and economic circumstances, which will themselves be changed by the new aesthetic humanity. In spite of those limitations, Lukács, like several Hegelian commentators, sees Schiller as moving away from the constraints imposed by Kant's epistemology and preparing the way for the change from subjective to objective idealism. Also, Schiller's attempts to stress the reciprocal action of sense on reason and vice versa indicates the beginnings of dialectical thinking. Lukács, however, sees Schiller's rejection of violent revolution and his attachment to Kant's system as excluding him from recognizing the nature of the historical process and as putting him firmly within the traditions of the eighteenth century. Lukács makes interesting reference in this connection to the Platonic elements in Schiller's thought, though he sees them as evidence of his aesthetics having strong pre-Kantian roots rather than seeing that Platonic and Neo-Platonic thought are also evident in Kant and, indeed, in Hegel. He also points to the ambiguity of Schiller's view of the position and role of art in social progress. On the one hand, art is in some sense the means of progress, but on the other, it exists in a separate realm and has a wholly nonutilitarian character. The fact that wholeness of personality is linked at various points in Schiller's aesthetics with leisure, with freedom from the exhausting effects of labor, lays him open, Lukács defensibly argues, to the charge of espousing a *l'art pour l'art* attitude. Lukács exonerates him conditionally, but purely because Lukács himself sees the evils of nineteenth-century capitalism as producing the decadent version of the same tendency.

Lukács's position received a modest challenge from Alexander Abusch, contributing an article on the *Ästhetische Briefe* to a volume of commemorative studies published in 1955. He acknowledges that Schiller renounced the idea of revolutionary struggle but stresses that he wanted to see the advent of true political freedom. Unable to reconcile those conflicting tendencies, Schiller saw the cultivation of the aesthetic as the only means of making an impact on his world without renouncing his humanist ideals. Abusch criticizes Lukács for not doing justice to the political implications of what Schiller wrote after 1794; in the mature dramas Abusch sees evidence of more complex intellectual engagement than in the earlier aesthetics or historiography with the nature of political action.

Another essay that clearly shows the influence of Lukács, though written after the time when it was possible to allude to him directly in the GDR because of his involvement in the Hungarian uprising in

1956, is that of Siegfried Seidel (1959). Seidel examines Schiller's uncertain position between subjective (Kantian) and objective (Hegelian) idealism and sees his propensity toward the former as deriving from his inability either to see social relations by analogy with nature (as did Goethe) or, as he predated Marx, to subject them to any objective kind of analysis. While his early dramas sound the note of social and political protest, his disappointment at their ineffectiveness in bringing change, intensified by the development of the French Revolution, caused him to plunge more fervently into the dualistic thinking of Kant's system. Seidel sees Schiller's notion of aesthetic education as flawed by being linked to a notion of beauty cut off from reference to reality. He sees *Über naive und sentimentalische Dichtung*, however, as evidence of a realistic turn in Schiller's theory, leading on in *Wallenstein* to a new realism in writing. He takes the treatise to indicate a revived interest on Schiller's part in mimetic theory and a move away from the contentlessness of his notion of beauty in the *Ästhetische Briefe*. In spite of the clear political and cultural prejudices evident in Seidel's essay, he is surely right that studies frequently neglect the later changes in Schiller's conception of the relation of form to content.

Claus Träger produced a more critical survey in the same year. Like Seidel and Lukács, he claims Schiller as a realist, led astray by Kant from the more concrete concerns of his early plays, but returning to them in the mid-1790s. Träger sees the concern of Kant and Schiller for the autonomy of art as regressive and Schiller's notion of its central position as an educative force as absurd and utopian and leading to the development of an "Elitetheorie" open to every kind of abuse and distortion. Yet Schiller never failed to see the poet's task as being political, in spite of his absurdly idealist position, and Träger sees his return to more practical poetic concerns in *Über naive und sentimentalische Dichtung* as an indication that he was too rooted in reality to continue his philosophical speculations any longer.

By the late 1960s GDR policy was changing, and emphasis on the cultural heritage was being reduced, not least because the impact of New Left thinkers such as Adorno and Marcuse in the West was producing criticism of a far more radical tendency than that of the East. Thus, the work of Eleonora Pfeifer (1974 and 1976) reads like a voice from the past in its stridently combative polemic against bourgeois criticism and its dogmatic insistence on the need to prove that Schiller, though writing before Marx, could be claimed as a thorough-going critic of capitalism. Claus Träger's introduction to his 1959 edition of Schiller's aesthetic writings was reprinted, with some changes, in the third edition in 1984. Although some of the more ideologically charged formulations have been moderated, the argument and approach are the same, and this lack of change is an indication of the static condition of GDR research on the subject after the first two decades.

While Theodor Adorno's attitude to Weimar Classicism was predominantly negative (his *Ästhetische Theorie* (1970) uses concepts such as *Schein* but in an utterly non-Schillerian sense) Herbert Marcuse's treatment of the *Ästhetische Briefe* in his study *Eros and Civilization: A Philosophical Enquiry Into Freud* (1955) builds on the image of Schiller as cultural critic and psychologist. Marcuse examines Freud's proposition that civilization is based on the permanent subjugation of human instincts in order to ask whether there might be a possibility of a nonrepressive civilization. This question leads him to an examination of the development of aesthetics in the eighteenth century. Though aesthetics as it arose in the late eighteenth century involved the cultural repression of contents inimical to the performance principle, the roots of the term aesthetic lie in the senses, and the foundation of aesthetics as an independent discipline invokes the inherent truth-values of the senses against their depravation under the force of the prevailing reality principle. Art, therefore, with its base in the sensual and the sensuous, is capable of challenging the prevailing principle of reason. From the standpoint of Kant's analysis, Schiller attempts to undo the sublimation of the aesthetic function. Only because beauty is a necessary condition of humanity can the aesthetic function play a decisive role in reshaping civilization. Marcuse sees Schiller as a forerunner of Marx in having developed a concept of alienation (a comment that would lead to many erroneous assumptions in the following decades). The notion of play is Schiller's way of envisaging a transformation of reality: "Aesthetic experience would arrest the exploitative productivity which made man into an instrument of labor" (154). The reconciliation of conflicting impulses would involve the removal of the tyranny of reason over sensuousness. The salvation of culture would involve the abolition of the repressive controls that civilization has imposed on sensuousness, so that Schiller can be seen as having sketched the elements of a reconciliation of the pleasure principle and the reality principle. Marcuse interprets Schiller as desiring and advocating freedom in reality, first an individual freedom and then as a transforming force in society. The Aesthetic State he sees as based on the principle that order is freedom only if it is founded on and sustained by the free gratification of the individual. Marcuse recognizes that Schiller did not concern himself with the cataclysmic changes in social structure that such a transformation would occasion, but he holds that that fact should not obscure the tendency of Schiller's thought, which was towards a nonrepressive order. Schiller implicitly recognizes, however, that only an order of abundance can bring about a nonrepressive culture, an insight that Marcuse identifies as the meeting point of the idealist and the materialist critiques of culture. Marcuse infers from this insight that production and distribution would need to be organized in such a manner that the least time is spent on making all necessities available to all members of society. Marcuse's analysis stresses the progressive in Schiller, assuming a basically democratic, even egalitarian tendency in his thought. It also rests on a primarily psychological interpretation of his theory of impulses or drives (*Triebe*). Marcuse can be seen as part of the general psychologizing tendency in criticism of Schiller's aesthetics, only in his case it is linked to a Marxist critique of existing socioeconomic relations. In common with a number of critics (for example Barnouw and Dewhurst and Reeves) who also stress the psychological approach, Marcuse sees in Schiller an upgrading of the sensuous. This, however, is a view for which a great deal of counter-evidence can be found. One can also see in Marcuse's analysis affinities with the Blochian notion of utopia, which seems to color some of the evaluations of the Aesthetic State from the late 1960s onward. Marcuse's approach is elaborated by Frederic Jameson (1971), who is discussed below in connection with *Über naive und sentimentalische Dichtung*.

A number of Western critics picked up the old Marxist line that Schiller had created a utopia as a flight from the intractable social and political realities of his day. An early contribution in the 1960s was Roy Pascal's appraisal in his article " 'Bildung' and the Division of Labour" in the festschrift for W.H. Bruford (1962). He looks not only at Schiller but also at Herder, Fichte, Wilhelm von Humboldt, and Goethe. He notes, as Lukács had, that the Scottish philosophers such as Smith and Ferguson had observed the effects of the division of labor and that in Germany the discussion assumed an urgent moral character: "That the social effects, so important for the Scotsmen, are neglected by the Germans, has its great and unhappy importance for later German culture" (25). In Schiller's treatment of the problem in the *Ästhetische Briefe* Pascal sees a unique intellectual passion and a personal involvement in the moral urgency of the task. His neglect of the social causes and ramifications of the division of labor and his concentration on the fulfillment of the whole self, however, are symptomatic of a particular kind of social and political quietism in the German intellectual tradition.

The impact of the New Left was evident in the ideological criticism of the new generation of scholars writing in the 1970s. In his *Theorie der Avantgarde* (1974) Peter Bürger took up the problematic nature of the notion of the autonomy of art and subjected it to scrutiny as the product of the conditions of bourgeois society. The development of this notion has the advantage, he argues, of sharpening the identity of the nonaristocratic classes but can have the disadvantage of taking art out of its social and political context. Schiller had the insight that human society is the result of a historical process and tried to conceive of the role of art in that process. Herbert Marcuse's prewar analysis *Über den affirmativen Charakter der Kultur* is the starting point for Hans-Heino Ewers's *Die schöne Individualität: Zur Genesis des bürgerlichen Kunstideals* [Beautiful Individuality: On the Genesis of the Bourgeois Ideal of Art](1978), a much more extended and negative critique than Bürger's. Ewers extrapolates from Marcuse's critique of the social origins of the cultural ideal to take in the theory of beauty, with the aim of showing that the concept of beauty as it emerged from the German idealist tradition developed away from being a political ideal to being a purely artistic one. Schiller and Hegel are the starting and finishing points for this process. Ewers sees in Schiller's appropriation of Kant a more radical and potentially dynamic relationship between beauty and morality. From the beginning of his study of Kant, Schiller reads the Kantian notion of freedom in aesthetic terms. His extension of the Kantian symbol-analogy idea of the relation of beauty and morality into the realm of the objective is seen by Ewers as a sign that he began with a potentially more direct conception of the interaction of the moral and aesthetic spheres. In the *Ästhetische Briefe* he sees Schiller as moving with Fichte's help toward an anticipation of the Hegelian notion of beauty. This philosophical development, however, also signals a progressive loss of political content in Schiller's aesthetics. Ewers perhaps reads too explicit a political content into Schiller's early aesthetics. Where the political becomes indisputably explicit in the *Ästhetische Briefe* it is marked by an almost immediate withdrawal. Schiller recognizes the circularity of the argument that beauty makes people free but that they have to be free before they can appreciate beauty. Though he can analyze the political dilemma of the age, however, he cannot solve it and retreats from the political level of argument, even though the fulfillment of "schöne Individualität" is logically the reproduction of that harmony at a suprapersonal level. Ewers sees *Über naive und sentimentalische Dichtung* as a further stage in the retreat from realizable political goals, for the solution that according to the *Ästhetische Briefe* would take more than a century is being pushed in the later treatise into an unattainable future.

After two decades of largely negative criticism from the left, Jürgen Habermas in *Der philosophische Diskurs der Moderne* [The Philosophical Discourse of Modernity] (1985) laid new emphasis on the progressive elements of Schiller's vision in the *Ästhetische Briefe*, seeing him in the radical tradition of aesthetics: "Schiller understands art as communicative reason which will be realized in the Aesthetic State of the future" (59; my translation). Schiller puts his faith in the public nature of art, in its power to create community and solidarity. Habermas clearly reaches back to ideas he first developed (though not specifically with regard to Schiller) in his influential *Strukturwandel der Öffentlichkeit* (1962; translated as *The Structural Transformation of the Public Sphere*, 1989). As in Marcuse's estimate, with which Habermas's has much in common, the utopian element is regarded not negatively but as the ultimate affirmation of art as the genuine embodiment of communicative reason.

Terry Eagleton in his *The Ideology of the Aesthetic* (1990), an examination of the linkage of aesthetics and political ideologies, also sees Schiller as part of the radical tradition in aesthetics. In Eagleton's view, at the heart of the development of the aesthetic debate from the late eighteenth century onward is the tension that the aesthetic "is at once . . . the very secret prototype of human subjectivity in early capitalist society, and a vision of human energies as radical ends in themselves which is the implacable enemy of all dominative or instrumentalist thought" (9). The idea of the autonomy of the work of art is closely linked to the emergence of art as a commodity in the marketplace, for art is now released from the various functions it traditionally fulfilled. Yet if the concept of autonomy serves the bourgeoisie as a useful model of subjectivity generally and serves the bourgeoisie's material aims, it also contains a vision of the self-determining nature of human powers that provides the basis (for example, in Marx) for revolutionary opposition to bourgeois utility.

Eagleton draws on Gramsci's notion of hegemony in his discussion of Schiller's aesthetics. He sees the development of aesthetics in eighteenth-century Germany as a response to the problem of political absolutism; aesthetic discourse is not a challenge to political authority, but it is symptomatic of ideological dilemmas inherent in absolutist power. Hence, he sees the *Ästhetische Briefe* as a kind of political allegory, reflecting that hegemonic struggle, in which the ambiguities of the argument are signs of genuine political dilemmas. It is characteristic of absolutism that reason has to assert its hegemony in the realm of taste and feeling — in other words over art. In Schiller's argument the Stofftrieb has to be broken down from within if human beings are to accept the rule of reason. Translating Schiller's terms into political equivalents (and thereby indirectly drawing attention to the political nature of Schiller's rhetoric), Eagleton sees his use of the term *aesthetic* as analogous to Gramsci's hegemony, but in a different key. Both men developed their ideas in the light of the collapse of revolutionary hopes. Thus: "The only politics that will hold is one firmly rooted in a refashioned "culture" and a revolutionized subjectivity'(106). But if the work is about the hegemony of reason over the senses, the relative status of the moral and the aesthetic (the old uncertainty of the *Ästhetische Briefe*) is indicative of a dilemma. The moral law, which the aesthetic is meant to serve, is a kind of absolute monarch that does not take cognizance of the individual. Only the aesthetic can generate a culture that creates cohesiveness among individuals, and such a culture necessarily has an oppositional character. Yet by virtue of the contentlessness of the aesthetic (in which the individual is simply potential) that opposition can only be potential rather than translated into any kind of action. This is Eagleton's analysis of why the treatise seems torn between elevating first the moral and then the aesthetic.

The Aesthetic State: Social and Political Implications

It was perhaps inevitable that World War II should spark off a certain amount of debate in Schiller studies about the German idea of freedom and Schiller's contribution to it. The *Ästhetische Briefe* loom large in this discussion. Leonard A. Willoughby refers in his article "Schiller on Man's Education to Freedom Through Knowledge" (1954) to a pamphlet of essays on Schiller by various exiled Germans that was published in 1942 by the Freier deutscher Kulturbund in Großbritannien. The tenor of the essays is liberal to left-wing, and in them Schiller is seen, among other things, as an "escapist into an illusory world of 'schöner Schein' " (164). Willoughby attempts to examine this objection. While acknowledging that Schiller rejected revolutionary change, he stresses that Schiller believed that people lacked the emotional drive rather than the intellectual insight to realize the ideals of the French Revolution and that the necessary psychological change would be brought about by aesthetic education. Thus, Willoughby takes seriously the political engagement of the *Ästhetische Briefe* and sees the work as a liberal rather than a utopian document. He finds Lukács's view incongruous, in particular the complaint about Schiller's limited insight into the forces governing social and political change. William Witte also takes up Lukács's challenge in his essay "Law and the Social Order in Schiller's Thought" (1955). He vindicates Schiller's ability to ask the vital questions, even if future commentators do not like the answer. He traces through the early work and up to the *Ästhetische Briefe* Schiller's continued emphasis on the need for social progress to be achieved by individuals, a continuity in Schiller's thought that is rarely highlighted. He reminds the reader that Schiller was quite aware that people's material needs had to be looked after if they were to have a chance of looking beyond their own immediate survival and of becoming receptive to aesthetic education.

Hans Reiss and Benno von Wiese took up the question of the status of the "ästhetischer Staat." Reiss (1956–1957) compares Schiller with Novalis in respect of the role of art in politics. He clearly shows the influence of Ilse Graham's central thesis, that Schiller's main preoccupation was with the proper sphere and application of aesthetic contemplation. He denies that the Aesthetic State is in any way a political ideal; it is, rather, a poetic idea that vindicates art and the poet and suggests "what the ideal community might look like and how the individual might play his part in it" (40). He then draws the vital distinction between Schiller and his younger Romantic contemporaries by pointing out that Schiller clearly delimited the aesthetic sphere, while for them it was unbounded in a way that for Schiller would indicate a dangerous confusion. Benno von Wiese attempted a vindication of the utopian element in the Aesthetic State in his article "Die Utopie des Ästhetischen bei Schiller" [The Utopia of the Aesthetic in Schiller] (1963). He stresses that the utopian idea reflects the eternal youth of the human imagination, even though the condition of life grants us only momentary restoration of our wholeness. Rather than being a flight from life's realities, Schiller's ideal realm can be imagined only when the constraints and tragedies of earthly life are fully acknowledged. Schein can be Schein only when it is not confused with the real. The function of the Aesthetic State is, thus, to provide us with a starting point for conceiving of a truly moral legislation.

The theory of aesthetic consciousness, on which the Aesthetic State is built, is subjected to a trenchant critique by the philosopher Hans-Georg Gadamer in his magisterial study of hermeneutics, *Wahrheit und Methode* (1962, translated as *Truth and Method*, 1975). Gadamer examines the way in which the human sciences as they emerged at the end of the eighteenth century maintained a humanist heritage that distinguishes them from the pure natural sciences and brings them close to extrascientific experiences, especially those associated with art. In the context of an examination of what is meant by "artistic truth," Gadamer examines the rise of the idea of artistic consciousness and questions its validity and the conception of art on which it is predicated. To Schiller he attributes the transformation of the transcendental idea of taste, as found in Kant, into a moral imperative. This transformation had far-reaching consequences, for a gulf opened up between art as Schein and nature. Art becomes a standpoint of its own. Hence, Schiller's plan in the *Ästhetische Briefe* changes to one where art is no longer the means but becomes the end; but that end is not freedom in reality but only in the realm of semblance. This move to aesthetic consciousness erodes the community of values implied in the word *taste*, which is linked to content in a way that aesthetic consciousness is not. The work of art becomes autonomous and thus detached from its historical context. Commissioned art drops in status, and the artist has to bear the burden of being a free agent, an ambiguous figure and yet a kind of secular savior. Gadamer's analysis of the dubiousness of the aesthetic consciousness sees Schiller's standpoint as a symptom rather than the cause of such a wide-ranging cultural development. His comments on autonomy have much in common with some of the critiques of Schiller's aesthetics produced in the 1970s, even though these are generally based on a Marxist analysis of cultural phenomena.

The 1970s saw intensive investigation of the social and political ramifications of Schiller's work, in part as the result of the impact of the radical questionings of the late 1960s. This development affected criticism of the dramas, in particular, but was also evident in approaches to the aesthetic essays. Rolf-Peter Janz's 1973 study of the aesthetics of Schiller and Novalis has as its main aim to trace what Novalis owed to Schiller and how he moved away from Schiller. Central to this investigation are the differing solutions given to the question of how the autonomy of art can be reconciled with its social function. Janz sees the insistence on the autonomy of art as a means of safeguarding it from being pressed into service by the church and the (feudal) state. Having propounded in his youth (for example, in *Die Schaubühne als eine moralische Anstalt betrachtet* [The Stage Considered as a Moral Institution]) the view that the theater had a moral and social task, Schiller, under Kant's influence, subsequently embraced a belief in the autonomy of art. Janz sees Schiller's motivation for engaging again with the question of the possible social function of art as lying in his observation of the events of the French Revolution. In returning to the idea of a social function conceived as aesthetic education in the *Ästhetische Briefe* his purpose was oppositional — to create through art the conditions for political freedom and to secure art against the danger of being a prop for the forces of reaction. The lack of clarity in the *Ästhetische Briefe* about whether art is the means or the end of aesthetic education Janz construes as the result of the problems of combining autonomy with social function, a stimulating though perhaps too schematic solution to that old problem.

The most substantial piece of writing on the *Ästhetische Briefe* in the 1970s was in Wolfgang Janke's *Historische Dialektik. Destruktion dialektischer Grundformen von Kant bis Marx* [Historical Dialectics: The Destruction of Basic Dialectical Forms from Kant to Marx] (1977), an investigation into the development and decline of dialectical systems based on various conceptions of human self-consciousness. The major part of the section Janke devotes to Schiller is a thorough analysis of the latter's transcendental method in the *Ästhetische Briefe* as a means of illuminating the claim Schiller makes at the beginning of the treatise that he is engaging in his argument with the issues raised by the French Revolution. Janke sees clearly the metaphysical nature of Schiller's argument and the ontological questions it raises. He begins by expounding the central dilemma in Schiller's analysis of the political problem: that of reconciling the need to change the political order while safeguarding the rights of the individual and guarding against the creation of a new tyranny that subordinates the individual to an idea of the whole. Schiller's transcendental method analyzes the antagonism between self and world, the absolute and the changing, and Janke expounds the precise meanings of Schiller's terms *Person, Zustand, Formtrieb, Stofftrieb* and *Spieltrieb*, showing that although the Kantian antinomy is resolved when both basic impulses are confined to their proper spheres, Schiller stresses how each is continually attempting to encroach on the realm of the other. Janke then explores the idea of reciprocal subordination as the means of overcoming this encroachment and the role and nature of the Spieltrieb in this process, giving attention to what he considers a peculiar feature of Schiller's dialectic, the notion of taking one step backwards to the state of determinability, out of which the restored harmony can emerge (an aspect also considered at length by Wilkinson and Willoughby in their edition of the *Ästhetische Briefe*, though with greater emphasis on the psychological than in Janke's account). The purpose of Janke's extended exegesis is to show clearly that for Schiller beauty is a necessary condition of being human. The dialectic Person-Zustand promises reconciliation within the individual of the fundamental division of existence, and beauty is the symbol of that reconciliation. Yet Janke is brave enough to go on from this clear exegesis to ask how this dialectic impinges on the political world — the question with which Schiller started — and how it can be reconciled with the rest of his theoretical works. Janke insists not on the political efficacy of the Aesthetic State but on its symbolic force, though he admits the difficulty presented by the fact that the world of Schein cannot be tied to political interests. He also insists that the *Ästhetische Briefe* have to be seen in conjunction with *Über naive und sentimentalische Dichtung* and with *Über das Erhabene*. Schiller stresses the violent opposition presented by nature to human fulfilment. The ennobled personality, a product of aesthetic education, may carry all fullness of being within, but in interaction with the external world it is the sublime that guarantees coherence of the personality in the face of nature as a blind force. Thus, the union of the sublime and the beautiful is self-contradictory. Janke breaks off at the point where one seeks an explanation of why Schiller should painstakingly construct a model and then seem to undermine it in other writings, but his careful analysis, which takes Schiller's transcendental argument seriously without arguing about Kantian terminology, leads in the direction of fruitful inquiry.

In "Property and Politics in Schiller's Theory of Aesthetic Education" (1980) Terry Holmes mounts a challenge both to liberal and to Marxist commentators who assume that all men are to be participants in the political community in the regenerated form that Schiller envisages. Still less does he accept the view that Schiller anticipated Marx in postulating a withering away of the state. Holmes examines the economic presuppositions behind the *Ästhetische Briefe*. Aesthetic education depends on leisure, which in turn depends on surplus production. In the *Ästhetische Briefe* "there exists between the "ownership" of aesthetic semblance and the ownership of tangible goods a closer relation than the metaphysical transference that operates here" (29). Holmes concedes the vital role that specialization plays in the sophistication of civilization: the surplus thereby produced maintains the cultural edifice. Holmes stresses that the equality existing in the Aesthetic State is purely figurative; in the earlier part of the treatise there is no call for social inequalities to be eradicated: "The metaphor of the Aesthetic State gives apt allegorical expression to Schiller's belief that the coincidence of freedom with order and right in public life depends on the aesthetic cultivation of balance and completeness in the individual" (36). While the Aesthetic State can be seen as a prerequisite for the emergence of the State of Reason (as in Letter 4) — a situation where the influence of a cultural elite gradually leads to political progress — nevertheless, the constituency of politically emancipated and participating citizens will still be restricted. Thus, Schiller's theory of aesthetic education does not waive any economic precondition for civic competence; Kant's property qualification seems to remain. This scrupulously argued piece provides a corrective to the trend of the early 1980s to magnify, possibly under the influence of Ernst Bloch, the utopian element in Schiller's thought. Walter Hinderer's "Utopische Elemente in Schillers ästhetischer Anthropologie" (1982) is an example of how difficult it is to extrapolate from Schiller's undoubted vision of a better world. Hinderer sees in Schiller a critique of social and political reality combined with a utopian idea linked to his ideal of human totality. Schiller's deep ambivalences about progress need to be addressed more squarely than they are here.

Philip J. Kain's *Schiller, Hegel and Marx: State, Society and the Aesthetic Ideal of Ancient Greece* (1982) aims to examine two interconnected themes: Marx's humanism and the relationship between the earlier and the later Marx. Schiller is considered in the light of this aim, and Kain argues that Marx's vision of the state comes progressively nearer to Schiller's, the ideal being an overcoming of alienation that would allow a condition characterized by the Greek aesthetic model. Kain asks how far Schiller succeeds in putting forward a convincing solution to fragmentation at the cultural, social and political levels. Schiller's aim is to transform labor and make it more like play, but Kain recognizes the problem of extending that condition beyond a small elite. He also recognizes the limitations of an argument based on the transformation of the individual personality, for it presupposes the power of such a transformation to remake all labor situations and transform them into fulfilling activity. Kain resists the conclusion that Schiller has set up a purely elitist construct in the Aesthetic State but concludes that Schiller's powers of analysis of the problem outstrip his ability find a solution. A similar recognition of the elitist implications of the Aesthetic State is found in Alfred Doppler's "Geschichtliche Situation und ästhetische Konzeption" [Historical Situation and Aesthetic Conception] (1982). Doppler focuses on the tension between the concept of aesthetic education, as the solution to the impasse of the historical situation represented by the French Revolution, and that of the autonomy of art, a notion that removes art from the sphere of experience for many people and turns it into the pursuit of an elite group. Doppler sees two possibilities of interpreting the role of art in society on the basis of the *Ästhetische Briefe*: either it is an elite activity in an isolated realm, or it creates a tension with the political realm and offers the alienated citizen some prospect of secular salvation. Doppler highlights the uncertainty of determining how the two realms relate to each other. A similar argument is pursued in detail, and from a sociological perspective, by Klaus Disselbeck in *Geschmack und Kunst* [Taste and Art] (1987); he sees both aesthetic education and the autonomy of art as concepts springing from the impulse to use art to solve social problems. The two concepts are, however, irreconcilable because they rest on conflicting assumptions about the structure of society.

In " 'Freiheit zu geben durch Freiheit' " ["Granting Freedom through Freedom"] (1982) Jeffrey Barnouw brings together his interest in Schiller's place in the empirical Enlightenment tradition with a conviction that Schiller's Aesthetic State constitutes a liberal ideal. In the triadic structure of the Dynamic, Ethical and Aesthetic States introduced at the end of the *Ästhetische Briefe* he sees a parallel to the structure of aesthetic experience arising out of the effect of the Spieltrieb on the two basic drives, the Formtrieb and the Stofftrieb. For Schiller, Barnouw argues, freedom in the individual is always anchored in empirical experience and to be expressed in action. Thus he aligns Schiller with the British empirical tradition begun by Hobbes and transmitted in Germany by Leibniz. Barnouw sees the difference in the meaning of freedom for Kant and Schiller as reflected by their notions of political freedom. Again, Schiller seems to him more of a liberal in the British tradition than Kant. Barnouw sees the Aesthetic State as resting on the principle of the balance of rights and duties, just as the aesthetic condition in the individual depends on the reciprocal action of the two basic drives. He sees in this more spontaneous interaction a more truly liberal concept than Kant's account of the motivation of citizens through need or deficiency. It is, of course, a huge and controversial leap from seeing the aesthetic condition as a paradigm for the Aesthetic State to seeing the latter as a paradigm for a political order. The distance between Kant and Schiller would seem to many to be much smaller than that between Schiller and the British tradition of political thought.

Josef Chytry also claims Schiller unequivocally for the liberal camp in his *The Aesthetic State: A Quest in Modern German Thought* (1989). Chytry claims for Schiller a "lifelong commitment to Commonwealthman political liberalism" (73). The *Ästhetische Briefe* are Schiller's way of harnessing that tradition for the defense of Weimar *Humanität*. Schiller's theory of play and his notion of Schein as manifested in social conduct imply in political terms a contractual theory whereby human beings acknowledge the freedom of others and the uniqueness of each natural object. Chytry points to Schiller's political quietism and his guardedness on the question of social inequality, seeing him as an adherent of the English constitutional model rather than of universal suffrage. He also asserts that Schiller's acceptance of art as a realm of Schein divorced from reality allowed him to explore the subversive elements of his thought in his dramas. Chytry's approach to Schiller constantly has the feel of someone judging by anachronistic standards — who *was* a democrat in the modern sense in the late eighteenth century? The English influences on Schiller's thought were filtered through the German intellectual tradition. Also, Chytry harmonizes Schiller's work by drawing on statements from writings often far apart in nature and in time and thus obscures the complexity of any attempt to infer stable political attitudes.

The Enlightenment Tradition and Anthropology

In the papers from a bicentenary colloquium published in 1960 in the *Jahrbuch der Deutschen Schillergesellschaft*, Elizabeth M. Wilkinson continued the series of articles that culminated in the dual-language edition of the *Ästhetische Briefe* that she and Leonard Willoughby published in 1967. In "Schiller und die Idee der Aufklärung" [Schiller and the Idea of Enlightenment] she addresses a subject that was to find renewed resonance in the 1980s, when the Enlightenment was becoming the focus for vigorous research and controversy. In 1959 she was writing in reaction to the tendency of the 1950s. For Wilkinson the essence of the Enlightenment lies in the mistrust of the autonomy of reason and of all operations of the mind detached from practical, empirical experience of the world. In Schiller she sees the same recognition that one dogmatism can easily follow the previous one. Schiller may look unlike an Enlightenment thinker in his attempt to vindicate the senses, but his criticism of the way reason is often used by modern people and his concern for freedom as a higher principle than reason are, Wilkinson suggests, preoccupations only superficially opposed to those of Enlightenment thinkers. While Schiller appears to anticipate the modern appreciation of culture as developing out of humanity's sensuous nature, this appreciation was also the legacy of the Enlightenment.

In the 1970s and 1980s Dieter Borchmeyer and Jeffrey Barnouw were most prominent in linking Schiller to various aspects of the Enlightenment tradition and in highlighting his mistrust of the dominance of reason divorced from experience. The impact of renewed interest in German reactions to the French Revolution during those decades is evident in their work. The empirical, experimental aspects of the Enlightenment also began to be rediscovered in the 1970s and this rediscovery led to new emphasis on "anthropology" in that specialized eighteenth-century sense, the conception of the whole person as a commerce of mind and body, spirit and matter. Kenneth Dewhurst and Nigel Reeves (1978) produced the first English translations of Schiller's medical dissertations, along with an extended commentary on the traditions of medical thought and contemporary theories on which they were based. Their survey of the impact of his medical training, with its highly speculative character, on his later works puts them in some measure in the tradition of Robert Sommer (1892), whose emphasis on the empirical, psychological aspects of Schiller's aesthetics also made him give prominence to the continuities in Schiller's thought from the Karlsschule days to the essays of the 1790s. Arguing that Schiller's "Triebe" in the *Ästhetische Briefe* are only superficially linked to Fichte's "Trieb" they suggest that the origin of Schiller's drives is in his early medical writing. This suggestion, however, ignores the essentially metaphysical nature of Schiller's argument. Similarly, while there is no denying the importance from his early work to his later of his concern for human totality, it is difficult to concur with Kwang-Myung Kim's claim in a doctoral dissertation for the University of Würzburg (1985) that Schiller's analysis of beauty appears to be "transcendental-metaphysical" but at bottom is "psychological-anthropological." This approach disregards the fact that Schiller's medical writings were anything but experimental in the modern scientific sense but were, on the contrary, highly speculative and pointed already to his metaphysical preoccupations, in spite of the clear psychological interest.

The anthropological approach was also boosted by the enthusiasm in the 1980s in Enlightenment scholarship for rediscovering the body and rehabilitating the senses, strong eighteenth-century preoccupations that had been neglected in favor of concentration on the rationalist tradition. Ulrich Tschierske's *Vernunftkritik und ästhetische Subjektivität: Studien zur Anthropologie Friedrich Schillers* [Critique of Reason and Aesthetic Subjectivity: Studies in Friedrich Schiller's Anthropology] (1988) stresses the aspects of Schiller's aesthetics that provide a corrective to the dominance of reason in the name of the claims of nature. Much of this can be seen as a variation on the old theme of harmony, with the additional element of opposition, and, as with that theme, the picture is not complete unless one pays attention to Schiller's unmistakable suspicion of the material world and his attachment to the ideal. Cathleen Muehleck-Müller recognizes the problem of the psychologizing tendency in the anthropological approach and offers an attempt at resolution in *Schönheit und Freiheit: Die Vollendung der Moderne in der Kunst. Schiller — Kant* [Beauty and Freedom: The Completion of Modernity in Art. Schiller — Kant] (1989), insisting that the anthropological concepts that underpin the broad notion of aesthetic education do not displace the transcendental foundation of Schiller's argument. His concept of the ethical remains essentially Kantian, but he uses that as a starting point from which to explore the anthropological ramifications of aesthetic experience. The author's central contention is that too little stress has been laid on the notion of aesthetic education, which she sees as running through all the theoretical writings, particularly those on tragedy, and which brings a coherence and continuity to those writings. The insights of Kant's *Critique of Judgment* were adapted by Schiller in such a way as to provide an anthropological basis for aesthetic education in common human experience.

Helmut Pfotenhauer (1991) examines the conflict between historical and anthropological approaches to art objects and the transcendental approach, a conflict he sees exemplified in Schiller's desire to adopt Kant's system and his simultaneous objection to the fact, as Schiller puts it in the Kallias letters, that Kant rates an arabesque more highly than the greatest human beauty. Pfotenhauer focuses on Schiller's references to classical statues as a means of combating the tendency in transcendental aesthetics for art to vanish into the unrepresentable. The statue is meant to provide evidence that what the mind cannot grasp systematically within a Kantian framework — that is, the possibility of a harmony between sense and reason — can actually find concrete expression in art. Pfotenhauer sees this discussion as something of an attempt to paper over the systematic cracks.

The Rhetorical Tradition

In 1959 *Euphorion* devoted a number to Schiller that included Herman Meyer's investigation of Schiller's philosophical rhetoric. Meyer's essay combines an examination of Schiller's appropriation of the rhetorical tradition with an attempt to define the role played by rhetoric and by Schiller's understanding of the importance of rhetoric in his own poetic work. Meyer's introduction, in which he examines side by side a passage from Kant's essay "What Is Enlightenment?" and the passage from the Augustenburg letters that was clearly influenced by that essay, clearly demonstrates the different handling of similar ideas. Looking back to the Karlsschule, Meyer traces the possible importance of Sulzer and Mendelssohn and later of Quintilian, whom Schiller read in the early 1790s and from whom, Meyer speculates, he may have gained encouragement to combine philosophical wisdom with eloquence. Schiller's notion of rhetoric Meyer sees as having been tested by the *Horen* project. In the Augustenburg letters Schiller sees the use of rhetoric as parallel in its effect to that of beauty — it frees the mind to consider the substance of the ideas being put forward. Yet Meyer sees a tension between the emphasis on free appreciation of form in the program of cultural ennoblement of *Die Horen* and the practical application of rhetoric as an agent of persuasion in that program. Fichte's objections to the *Ästhetische Briefe* (that they were brilliantly written, but afterwards one did not know what one had read) seemed to Schiller to stand on its head what he was actually trying to achieve. He elaborates this contention in *Von den notwendigen Grenzen beim Gebrauch schöner Formen* [On the Necessary Limits in the Use of Beautiful Forms] (1802), seeing rhetoric as part of the appeal of the work to the whole human being — beauty and logic working in harmony.

Focusing on the practice of rhetoric in her Special Taylorian Lecture of 1959 in Oxford, 'Schiller - Poet or Philosopher?'(1961), Elizabeth M. Wilkinson attempts to rescue Schiller from the charge that poetry interfered with his philosophy (a charge based on Schiller's own comments, of course). She sketches some of his characteristic structural and rhetorical devices — tautology, chiasmus, and circular structure — and thus anticipates the analysis of her later dual-language edition. Her verdict is that far from his philosophical development being impeded, his artist's gifts were integrated into his philosophy to expand his philosophical expressiveness.

It was not until the 1970s that Meyer's essay bore fruit in renewed attention to Schiller's place in the rhetorical tradition. In the context of a discussion of Goethe's *Wilhelm Meisters Lehrjahre* in 1963 Heinz Otto Burger had pointed to the fact that Schiller's notions of grace and Schein could be related to the courtly tradition. Gerd Ueding's 1971 monograph *Schillers Rhetorik* examines Schiller's appropriation of the classical rhetorical traditions, including the legacy of Castiglione and Shaftesbury, but rather than supporting Burger's implication that the adoption of such an ideal was regressive, Ueding sees Schiller as creating in his approach to aesthetics a "Citoyen-Ideal," that unites the civic virtue of the bourgeoisie with the best of the aristocratic tradition, so overcoming the alienation of the educated middle class. Ueding examines all of Schiller's key aesthetic concepts in the light of this classical and courtly tradition and thereby reduces the importance of Kantian philosophy as an influence. He argues, for example, that Schiller's notion of taste, while embracing Kant's, also includes sociability and the creation of a way of life. The study effectively illuminates another aspect of the confluence of ancient and modern in Schiller's work, whether or not one accepts the overarching argument concerning aristocracy and bourgeoisie.

In *Tragödie und Öffentlichkeit — Schillers Dramaturgie im Zusammenhang seiner ästhetisch-politischen Theorie und die rhetorische Tradition* [Tragedy and the Public — Schiller's Dramaturgy in the Light of his Aesthetic-Political Theory and the Rhetorical Tradition] (1973), Dieter Borchmeyer takes up Jürgen Habermas's idea of the creation of a public sphere in the later eighteenth century that served as a forum for the exploration of the concerns of an enlightened intelligentsia and looks at how, in theory and in practice, Schiller contributes to the formation of such a public sphere. In the process he produces one of the most wide-ranging attempts to link Schiller's aesthetics to his dramatic practice. Borchmeyer sees the notion of aesthetic education as an attempt to bridge the gulf between individual and community in the public realm as well as a means of reconciling reason and senses in the individual. Schiller's belief in art as a transforming and civilizing power draws on the rhetorical tradition but reinterprets it in the light of contemporary needs. Thus, in reintroducing the chorus in *Die Braut von Messina* [The Bride of Messina] (1803), as Schiller explains his purpose in his prefatory essay "Über den Gebrauch des Chors in der Tragödie," he is attempting to find something of a modern equivalent to the public forum created by ancient drama. Borchmeyer interprets the *Ästhetische Briefe* from a liberal humanist perspective. For Schiller the decline and demise of the ancien regime was a political inevitability. Yet he recognized that the disappearance of a visible public arena from the individual's direct experience was both a political and an aesthetic problem. Both political and individual life had to acquire an aesthetic character, and Borchmeyer explores the function of taste as an individual and as a social phenomenon. These themes are developed by flexible and wide-ranging reference to the essays on aesthetics and on tragedy.

In the 1980s Borchmeyer explored in a series of articles the role of the rhetorical tradition in Schiller's response to the course taken by the French Revolution. Schiller's complaint in the Augustenburg letters

and in the *Ästhetische Briefe* is that theoretical culture, the enlightenment of the mind, has not been accompanied by "practical culture,"
which makes the heart receptive to the convictions of the mind.
Borchmeyer sees this notion of practical culture as being essentially the
same as aesthetic culture, and as being linked to the rhetorical tradition,
in that rhetoric formerly also had the function of persuading not only
the mind but also the heart; and thus rhetoric can be seen as in some
measure analogous to aesthetic education. By this analogy Borchmeyer
highlights Schiller's critique of the one-sidedness of Enlightenment rationalism. Yet distinctions are also illuminating. Borchmeyer (1984)
points out that in the Aristotelian tradition the realms of practical wisdom and theoretical knowledge were kept apart, whereas in Schiller's
notion of aesthetic education practical culture is the preparatory phase
for theoretical culture. In consequence, aesthetic education means that
that education is emptied of specific contents; it is based not on knowledge but on Schein. Borchmeyer sees Schiller's response to the French
Revolution as drawing a distinction between its principles and its practice. He repudiated the latter but not the former and suggested aesthetic education as a way of achieving political change by
nonrevolutionary means. In an illuminating discussion of Burke and
Schiller as critics of the French Revolution (1983) Borchmeyer sees in
Schiller's practical culture the equivalent of Burke's appeal to rhetoric
and the Aristotelian practical disciplines. Schiller's dualism, however, he
sees as cutting him off from the old rhetorical tradition and from the
empirical tradition in general. In addition, though Burke was more
hostile to the principles of the French Revolution than Schiller, his con-
servatism allowed for natural change, whereas Schiller's theoretical support for the State of Reason at the beginning of the *Ästhetische Briefe*
gives way by the end to the nebulous fictive construct of the Aesthetic
State.

One of the outstanding pieces of work on the *Ästhetische Briefe* of
the 1980s was a dissertation written for the University of London and
published until 1981, some ten years after submission, as *Schiller and
"Alienation."* Victoria Rippere mounts a challenge to the vague but
widespread notion current in the 1960s that Schiller was the father of
the concept of alienation in Marx's sense, a claim based on the *Ästhetische Briefe* and in particular on his portrait of the age and the fragmentation of the individual as a result of the division of labor. Rippere is
concerned to correct a doubly misleading picture, one that credits
Schiller with originality where she sees none and fails to recognize the
originality there is. She traces the origin of the connection between

Schiller and alienation to Heinrich Popitz's *Der entfremdete Mensch* [The Alienated Person] (1953), in which Popitz presents Schiller as one of a number of writers who touched on aspects of problems later taken up by Marx. The already fairly imprecise analysis was subsequently adopted and blunted by commentators such as Marcuse until any sense of the specific context of Schiller's portrait of the age had been lost. Apart from being a modish preoccupation (the author delayed publication for this reason), the alienation debate, she contends, ignores the function of commonplaces in the rhetorical strategy of any portrait such as Schiller's portrait of the age. Too often critics have taken that portrait to be an imitation of nature. Rather "it is a perceptual schema that has become more and more conventional over the years" (98). She proceeds to show how the late-eighteenth-century milieu was saturated with concepts of "alienation" and produces detailed and illuminating comparisons with a range of German, British, and French writers to strengthen her contention that Schiller was picking up on commonplaces current at the time and adapting them for his own purposes. Reminding us that Schiller uses a rhetor in the work, she shows how he employs various rhetorical strategies, including what she calls "minimal allusion" — the technique of toning down or paraphrasing the usual wording of some piece of conventional wisdom — to create a sense of consensus among the readership and thus a basis on which to encourage acceptance of the project of aesthetic education. The use of commonplaces is also a means by which to convince the reader that solutions already tried are inadequate.

Todd C. Kontje's study *Constructing Reality: A Rhetorical Analysis of Friedrich Schiller's Letters on the Aesthetic Education of Man* (1987) brings postmodernist perspectives to the investigation of the rhetorical strategy of the work. Kontje seeks to relate the form of the treatise to its historical setting in a more precise way than had been previously attempted. He sees a direct relation between the content of Schiller's theory of aesthetic education, which involves the attempt to link autonomous aesthetics to his historical situation, and the rhetorical strategy employed to relate this content to the reader. He discusses Schiller's concern to find an adequate language and style of presentation for his philosophy, rejecting both Lutz's notion of the two distinct layers of argument and Wilkinson's and Willoughby's theory that the strategy of the piece is to create a circularity of structure that reflects the operation of the psyche. Rather, Kontje sees the "schöne Schreibart" as being the correlate to the Spieltrieb, mediating the treatise by evoking aesthetic experience through the rhetoric of the text.

Rooted as it is in the conventions of the polite society Schiller knew, with its rigid hierarchies, the strategy as a method of boosting social and political change threatens, in the author's view, "to become a futile exercise in the self-confirmation of an already existing group of individuals" (128).

Über naive und sentimentalische Dichtung

The main German editions of Schiller's works since 1945 were discussed in an earlier section of this chapter. *Über naive und sentimentalische Dichtung* was made more accessible to non-German readers by several editions and translations. Robert Leroux matched his dual-language French-German edition of the *Ästhetische Briefe* with one of *Über naive und sentimentalische Dichtung* in 1946. His introduction shows him less at home with a work on poetics. He begins with a long and convoluted account of the idea of nature in the work that fails to communicate the interest and importance of the essay. William F. Mainland's Blackwell edition of the German text (1957), is similarly not geared to the reader who seeks initial orientation, though in the course of the introduction he gives useful background information on the idea of the naive, the discussion of genius, and the meaning of Schiller's *sentimentalisch*. Julius A. Elias's English translation of the essay along with *Über das Erhabene* (1966) was used by H.B. Nisbet in his useful volume *German Aesthetic and Literary Criticism* (1985) and furnished with helpful notes and a compact general introduction. Helen Watanabe O'Kelly also added a concise introduction and notes to her careful translation of 1981. In spite of this increased accessibility and the postwar expansion of Schiller criticism, treatments of this work are still sparse. The nearest one comes to a continuing debate is the response in the GDR to Lukács's essay on the question of Schiller's realism and the discussion of the 50s and 60s of Schiller's position with regard to Friedrich Schlegel and the poetics of German Romanticism.

Georg Lukács's essay "Schillers Theorie der modernen Literatur" was published for the first time in 1947 in the collection *Goethe und seine Zeit* [translated as *Goethe and his Age*, 1968]. Lukács's sustained concern with the nature of realism comes to the fore. He focuses first on the classical ideal as it came to be interpreted by Weimar Classicism. In *Über naive und sentimentalische Dichtung* Schiller contrasts the realism and objectivity of Homer with the "sentimental" Ariosto. In that essay and later in "Über den Gebrauch des Chors in der Tragödie" he recognizes that the Greek world and its simple realism are gone forever and that the modern writer has to face the challenge of how to manage the gulf that opens up in his imagination between the real and the ideal. Schiller rejects a mere photographic realism, maintaining that it does not penetrate to the reality beneath the surface. While Lukács cannot applaud Schiller's insistence that modern writers have to find ways of incorporating ideal content in their work, he does see his distinction between "wahre Natur" [true nature] and "wirkliche Natur" [actual nature] as providing a starting point for the consideration of the problem of realism. Schiller meant by "true nature" the ideal contours of life, whereas for Lukács the poet's task is to uncover the determinants of modern life. Nevertheless, Schiller recognizes that detail is only a means to an end, that art can show the deeper level of reality only indirectly since it is not given directly to our experience. He also sees Schiller as an important forerunner of Hegel in beginning to recognize that the conditions of modern bourgeois society have to be the starting point for any theory of literature, even though his conclusion was that in a world dominated by production the flame of art can be tended only among those who can stand apart from those conditions. Lukács's emphasis on Schiller's realism was, as we have seen in the work of Seidel and Träger, influential in the GDR. Among Western critics, however, it failed to generate much response.

In the 1950s American critics provided a helpful overview for the new reader. In *The Later Eighteenth Century* (1955), the first volume of his *History of Modern Criticism 1750–1950*, René Wellek begins his magisterial survey at the point at which the neoclassical system began to disintegrate, with the consequent emergence of some of the issues that have dominated criticism ever since. His approach is to try to achieve a balance between aesthetics and criticism, defined as expression of taste without philosophical underpinning. Hence, though he gives a brief review of the *Ästhetische Briefe*, his main attention when he comes to Schiller is focused on *Über naive und sentimentalische Dichtung* and on the more practical aspects of the work rather than on its speculative base. He gives a lucid summary of the essay in its historical context, acknowledging Schiller's difficulty in combining "a typology of literature with a philosophy of its history and a concrete critical application to particular figures and ages" (236), and points to some of the logical and terminological shifts. Although M. H. Abrams makes only brief references to the essay in his seminal work *The Mirror and the Lamp: Romantic Theory and the Critical Tradition* (1953) he nevertheless illuminates impressively the context in which Schiller's poetics arose and allows the reader to see that poetics in a wider European, as opposed to purely German, setting.

The debate on Schiller's relationship to Friedrich Schlegel was taken up first in the postwar period by Hans Eichner. In 1955 he gave a concise account, "The Supposed Influence of Schiller's *Über naive und sentimentalische Dichtung* on F. Schlegel's *Über das Studium der griechischen Poesie*", in which he challenged on the basis of both internal and external evidence the old claim that Schlegel changed the end of his essay in the light of Schiller's. He traces the rhetorical strategy of Schiller's essay, pointing out how Schlegel's praise for the moderns at the end is still based on the degree to which they have found a successful style of imitation of the ancients. The Vorrede [Preface], he confirms, was indeed written under the influence of Schiller's essay. In 1958 Richard Brinkmann sought to clarify further the relationship between Schiller's concept of the "sentimental" and Friedrich Schlegel's notion of the "interesting" in the latter's study of Greek poetry. He makes the important observation that at this stage the modern for Schlegel is summed up by the word *characterless*, by which he means purely individual and lacking universality, whereas for Schiller "sentimental" writing is less defined by its pursuit of the individual than by its tendency to distort the individual in the light of an overriding idea. Nor does the "interesting", for Schlegel, have any implications about the reflection of an ideal, whereas Schiller's notion of the naive certainly strongly implies a moral contrast as well as an aesthetic one underlying the gulf between real and ideal. Brinkmann sees Schiller's reasons for rejecting Schlegel in an awareness on Schiller's part that Schlegel's method of seeking the transcendental in the totality of history amounts to a loss of the transcendental altogether.

In 1967 Hans Robert Jauss looked at the contribution made by Schiller and Friedrich Schlegel to the old "Querelle des Anciens et des Modernes." In doing so he was correcting the clichés about literary periodization that cut off Weimar Classicism from its roots in the Enlightenment and was thus anticipating an important trend in criticism of the 1980s. The answers Schiller and Schlegel give to the question of the relative merits of ancient and modern writers bear the imprint of the intellectual impact of the Enlightenment, an age during which the Greek achievement became increasingly idealized and burdened with modern sentiment but also appeared more and more clearly as part of an irrecoverable past. Schiller, Jauss argues, helped Schlegel out of the impasse of his negative appraisal of the modern in relation to the Greeks by helping him to see ancient and modern literature as part of a continuum and within a theory of historical development in which the irrecoverability of the Greek ideal can be set against the larger backcloth of necessary change and progress. A postscript to the ancient-modern, Schiller-Schlegel debate is provided in the essay by Leonard P. Wessell, the title of which, "Schiller and the Genesis of German Romanticism" (1971), is a conscious allusion to A.O. Lovejoy's famous essay of the same name. Wessell sees Schiller's historical framework for *Über naive und sentimentalische Dichtung* as a means of solving the problem of the incompatibility of his notions of the beautiful and the sublime, which are conceptually related to the naive and the sentimental. Thus, the two ideals, in the first of which beauty represents a higher value than the purely moral and in the second of which beauty becomes inferior to morality, are presented as appropriate to different epochs of human development. Wessell challenges Brinckmann's view that Schiller's "sentimental" by its moral emphasis is fundamentally different from Schlegel's "interesting".

Jost Hermand's "Schillers Abhandlung *Über naive und sentimentalische Dichtung* im Lichte der Popularphilosophie des 18. Jahrhunderts" [Schiller's Treatise *On Naive and Sentimental Poetry* in the Light of the Popular Philosophy of the Eighteenth Century] (1964) takes up the impetus given by Benno von Wiese in his monograph of 1959 and in volumes 20 and 21 of the Nationalausgabe. Emphasizing the eclectic nature of the treatise and denying any strong Kantian influence on the central pair of terms, Hermand looks at the development of the term *naive*, tracing the possible influence of Mendelssohn, Sulzer, Weisse, Rousseau, and Garve and examining the ways in which the idea of the schöne Seele, a concept closely allied to that of "das Naive der Gesinnung," has its roots in the typical popularphilosophisch intermingling of ethics and aesthetics. While he recognizes the sentimental as Schiller's own concept without the same history as the naive, he traces the possible influence of Garve and Christian Meiners on Schiller's recognition of the gulf that separates moderns from the Greeks. Hermand goes on to challenge the idea that, in turning to speculative thought, Schiller was setting himself up as an apostle of aesthetic values, for having used the treatise to clarify his own ideas he turned decisively away from speculative thought and experimented in his poetic work with different solutions to the naive-sentimental problem. The strange notion of a higher level of reconciliation that unites the naive and the sentimental is explained by Hermand not in logical terms but rather as the product of Schiller's desire to separate himself from the one-sidedness of the sentimental.

Schiller's view of nature in the treatise has provoked a variety of responses. The changing meanings of the term in the treatise are analyzed by Olive Sayce (1962), who sees the discrepancies as arising primarily from the needs of an argument based on antitheses. George A. Wells (1966) is disturbed by Schiller's use of the word *nature* to mean different things. For him, "the essay is vitiated by its optimistic and unhistorical view of human nature, by its erroneous statements about the Ancient Greeks, by the elaborate apparatus of psychological faculties and capacities that it posits, and by the ambiguity of some of the key words on which the argument depends" (491). Wells's essay is vitiated by his inability to see beyond these undoubted problems to the central critical themes, which are not, as he believes, an explanation of why Homer fails to wax lyrical over the sunset but an exploration of the modern poetic consciousness. Wells, nevertheless, at least exposes clearly some of the interpretative problems. More recently (1986), Wolfgang Marx has argued that Schiller's "sentimental" philosophy has naive components. He makes this claim on the grounds that Schiller sought and found in nature a common foundation for his two types of poetic consciousness. But this discovery required him to reject the transcendental idea of nature proper to his philosophical system in favor of nature as *natura naturans.* This move, for Marx, constitutes a leap from the constraints of a transcendental system into the fairy-tale world of nature as innocent perfection. The anthropological argument emerges again here, for Marx sees nature as having to provide the possibility of healing human fragmentariness in Schiller's scheme. One feels that there is more cleverness than insight in this approach, which does not take account of the mobility of Schiller's use of the term *nature* in the treatise.

On the question of Schiller's categories there have been two main contributions. In the commemorative number of the *Jahrbuch der Deutschen Schillergesellschaft* in 1960 Wolfgang Binder attempted, by using the instance of the categories naive and sentimental, to sum up the problem of the relationship of Schiller's aesthetics to his creative work, and to his dramas in particular, and thus to mediate between those who see in the dramas examples of aesthetic categories and those who deny the relevance of the aesthetics to the dramas. The problem is raised by Schiller himself, who refers in letters to some of his own dramatic characters as naive. Binder stresses that naive and sentimental are "transzendental-ontologisch." They are not, in the first instance, categories drawn from psychology or anthropology, let alone from poetics, and they can be transferred to other realms only after they have been transformed into the equivalent historical or anthropological frame-work — and then only as a regulative function. The most influential essay of the 1970s on the treatise was Peter Szondi's "Das Naive ist das Sentimentalische: Zur Begriffsdialektik in Schillers Abhandlung *Über naive und sentimentalische Dichtung*" [The Naive is the Sentimental: On the Conceptual Dialectics in Schiller's Treatise *On Naive and Sentimental Poetry*] (1972), the second part of the title pointing to the fact that Szondi sees Schiller's argumentation in the treatise as drawing on Kant and anticipating Hegel. He reexamines the relationship of the naive to the sentimental, concluding that the sentimental is not the opposite of the naive but rather the attempt to regain the naive by means of the reflective understanding and the pursuit of the ideal. Szondi sees the treatise as springing from three sources: Schiller's own poetic work, his need to clarify his position vis à vis Goethe, and his appropriation of Kantian principles. Examining Schiller's famous birthday letter to Goethe, Szondi explores the problem Schiller faced in accounting consistently for Goethe's different type of poetic consciousness. The notion expressed in the treatise that the naive poet in a sentimental age can take up sentimental subject matter indicates that the sentimental is not the opposite of the naive but is the third stage of a dialectic, in which the reflective understanding is the second term. This solution Szondi attributes to Schiller's appropriation of Kant's historical thinking. The *Critique of Pure Reason*, alluded to in an important footnote in the treatise, provided Schiller with a triadic structure of historical progress that allowed him to place naive and sentimental in a dialectical relationship. Szondi may overstate the importance of the footnote and thus suggest that it is responsible for a more fundamental change of conception than is actually the case, mobile though Schiller's terminology and argument undoubtedly are. Also, Schiller himself states that it is "die Kunst," art in the specialized sense of artificiality, that divides man, and so this concept (admittedly, clearly linked with that of the reflective understanding) is more consistently the second term of the dialectic, in spite of what he says in the late footnote. Szondi nevertheless throws light on the dynamics of Schiller's argument.

While comprehensive studies of the treatise were generally lacking in the 1970s, that decade saw the emergence of renewed interest in Schiller's theory of the idyll. This interest gave rise to studies such as Gerd Sautermeister's *Idyllik und Dramatik im Werk Friedrich Schillers* (1971), which traced the impact of the notion of the idyll on Schiller's later dramatic practice. The most substantial piece of work on the notion of the idyll as developed in *Über naive und sentimentalische*

Dichtung came from Gerhard Kaiser in his collection of essays *Wandrer und Idylle: Goethe und die Phänomenologie der Natur in der deutschen Dichtung* (1977), in which he compares Schiller's and Goethe's engagement with the idyll. He emphasizes in particular the historical progression on which the notion of the idyll is based, drawing attention to the influence of Kant's speculative history in his *Conjectural Beginning of Human History* and to the dual nature of the idyll concept, the Arcadian and the Elysian idyll, the former reflecting an age of precivilized innocence, the latter the resolution of the tensions created by humanity's journey from innocence through sophistication to restored harmony. In this respect Kaiser sees Schiller as the heir to Vergil's fourth *Eclogue*, with its eschatological tendency, as well as contributing to the secularization of Christian myth in the transformation of Fall and Redemption into the necessary progression of history. The real challenge of the idyll lies, of course, in showing how such a theory could ever be manifest in poetry.

Perhaps the most stimulating contribution of the 1970s came from Frederic Jameson, who draws on the essay in his discussion of the functioning of a "Marxist hermeneutic", which he defines as "a political discipline" that "provides the means . . . of preserving the concept of freedom itself" (86). Emphasizing the political dimension of the *Ästhetische Briefe*, he is unusual in seeing *Über naive und sentimentalische Dichtung* as a demonstration of their claim that only through beauty can we find the way to freedom:

> Schiller descends into the detail of the work of art itself, there teaching us to see the very technical construction of the work as a *figure* of the struggle for psychic integration in general, to see in images, quality of language, type of plot construction the very figures (in an imaginary mode) of freedom itself. (91)

Looking back to Marcuse's elaboration of Schiller's ideas on the progress of the state in the light of Freud's pleasure principle (see above, "Marxist Approaches"), Jameson sees the categories of the naive and the sentimental as illuminated by the Freudian theory of memory; the memory of psychic wholeness and gratification is in Schiller's essay expressed as a speculative history of the origins of civilization: "Schiller wishes to determine . . . how man's psyche would have had to have been constructed for a genuinely free and harmonious personality to become one day a real possibility" (115). Jameson's discussion includes stimulating references to Romanticism, Surrealism and American New Criticism. His tendency to run together the distinct speculative histories underlying the *Ästhetische Briefe* and *Über naive und sentimentalische Dichtung* is, however, potentially misleading.

Schiller's treatment of the Greeks, an issue central to *Über naive und sentimentalische Dichtung*, has attracted periodic attention. Like Schiller's view of nature, this topic often seems to yield less than one might expect, as the relevant chapters in the works of Eliza Butler and Walter Rehm in the 30s already demonstrated. In a volume of *Commemorative American Studies* (1959), Henry Hatfield, in anticipation of the chapter in his book-length study *Aesthetic Paganism*, asked in "Schiller, Winckelmann, and the Myth of Greece" how far Schiller continued and in what respects he opposed the tradition of Winckelmann. He concludes that Schiller's response to the myth of Greece was stimulating and productive, yet his affinity to Winckelmann and the Greeks was not great. A more fruitful approach by far is that of Albert Meier (1985) who begins with the inconsistency of Schiller's presentation of the Greeks from his historical lectures to the aesthetic essays and analyzes the argumentative strategies that produce the variations. In the *Ästhetische Briefe* Meier sees Schiller as trying to combine Rousseau's cultural pessimism with a belief in the possibility of a harmonious culture. In *Über naive und sentimentalische Dichtung* Schiller tries to combine a Herderian view of the Greeks with Kant's use of the notion of "Antagonism" to explain historical progress and the resulting inconsistency as the result of the incompatibility of these two approaches to history. Bernd Fischer's recent article "Goethes Klassizismus und Schillers Poetologie der Moderne: *Über naive und sentimentalische Dichtung*" (1994) presents the essay as a response to the theoretical problems inherent in Goethe's classicizing poetics. Goethe's adherence to them makes his poetics of the 1790s resistant to and unable to account for the modern. Schiller's treatise can be seen as an attempt to accommodate and transcend Goethe's poetics. The philosophy of history — the postulation of an absolute reconciliation of all conflicts — underpinning *Über naive und sentimentalische Dichtung* allows the complementarity of the naive and the sentimental. Fischer sees Schiller as having been unable to pursue the Romantic tendencies of his theory, lest collaboration with Goethe should become impossible.

Postscript

FROM THIS SURVEY it will be clear that on many major issues in Schiller's aesthetics opinion is as divided as ever. What is no longer in dispute is that these essays contributed some seminal ideas to their field and deserve detailed attention as part of the German idealist tradition in aesthetics. This study shows the interaction of philosophical and literary approaches. If Schiller's aesthetics were at first neglected, it was the work of philosophers, above all, that restored their status. Yet at the same time the immense prestige of Kant in Germany meant that Schiller's achievement could not be fully explored until the Kantian influence was seen in a wider context and the texts themselves were subjected to literary, as well as philosophical, analysis. Striking is the increasingly marked politicization of that process since 1945. In the nineteenth century it was Schiller's plays and poems that caused him to be exploited for political purposes, while the aesthetics were relatively untouched. Since 1945 it has been the criticism of the aesthetics, as much as, if not more than, that of his plays, that has reflected broader ideological tensions as well as the critical fashions of the field of German studies.

In spite of heated disputes and a steady stream of new criticism some areas remain underresearched. *Über naive und sentimentalische Dichtung* is still a neglected work, whose exact relation to Schiller's other essays requires further definition. His theory of the sublime has not been thoroughly explored in the light of recent debates on that concept. The gendering of aesthetic categories in the essays has, as yet, been treated only cursorily. It is to be hoped that scholars will take up these challenges and thus continue the debate on these most fascinating but elusive works.

Works Consulted

Schiller's principal writings on aesthetics

1792 *Über den Grund des Vergnügens an tragischen Gegenständen. Neue Thalia*, no. 1. Republished in *Kleinere prosaische Schriften*, volume 4. Leipzig: Göschen, 1802.

1792 *Über die tragische Kunst. Neue Thalia*, no. 2. Republished in *Kleinere prosaische Schriften*, volume 4. Leipzig: Göschen, 1802.

1792 *Vom Erhabenen. Neue Thalia* nos 3 and 4. Republished in a shortened version as *Über das Pathetische* in *Kleinere prosaische Schriften* volume 3. Leipzig: Göschen, 1801.

1793 *Kallias oder über die Schönheit*. Preparatory letters written 25 January and 8, 18, 19, 23, and 28 February. *Schillers Briefwechsel mit Körner: Von 1784 bis zum Tode Schillers*. Berlin: Veit, 1847.

1793 *Über Anmut und Würde. Neue Thalia*, no. 2. Republished in *Kleinere prosaische Schriften*, volume 2. Leipzig: Göschen, 1800.

1795 *Über die ästhetische Erziehung des Menschen in einer Reihe von Briefen. Die Horen* 1, nos 1, 2, 6. Republished in *Kleinere prosaische Schriften*, volume 3. Leipzig: Göschen, 1801.

1795 *Von den notwendigen Grenzen des Schönen. Die Horen* 1, no. 9. Combined with *Über die Gefahr ästhetischer Sitten* and republished as *Über die notwendigen Grenzen beim Gebrauch schöner Formen* in *Kleinere prosaische Schriften*, volume 4. Leipzig: Göschen, 1802.

1795 *Über die Gefahr ästhetischer Sitten. Die Horen* 1, no. 11. Combined with *Von den notwendigen Grenzen des Schönen* and published under the title *Über die notwendigen Grenzen beim Gebrauch schöner Formen* in *Kleinere prosaische Schriften*, volume 4. Leipzig: Göschen, 1802.

1795–96 *Über naive und sentimentalische Dichtung. Die Horen* 1, nos 11 and 12 and *Die Horen* 2, no. 1. Later published in *Kleinere prosaische Schriften* 2. Leipzig: Göschen, 1800.

1796 *Über den moralischen Nutzen ästhetischer Sitten. Die Horen* 2, no.3.

1801 *Über das Erhabene*. In *Kleinere prosaische Schriften*, volume 3. Leipzig: Göschen.

Selected editions and translations

1844 *Friedrich Schiller: Philosophical and Aesthetic Letters.* Translated by J. Weiss. London: Chapman.

1849 *Correspondence of Schiller with Körner, Comprising Sketches and Anecdotes of Goethe, the Schlegels, Wieland and other Contemporaries.* 3 vols. London: Bentley.

1861 *Schiller's Complete Works. Translated.* Edited by C.J. Hempel. 2 vols. Philadelphia: Kohler.

1871 *Ästhetische Schriften.* Edited by Reinhold Köhler. Volume 10 of *Schillers sämmtliche Schriften: Historisch-kritische Ausgabe*, edited by Karl Goedeke. Stuttgart: Cotta.

1875 *Essays Aesthetical and Philosophical; Including the Dissertation on the "Connection between the Animal and Spiritual in Man".* Translator anon. Bohn's Standard Library. London: Bell.

1904–05 *Philosophische Schriften.* Edited by Oskar Walzel. Volumes 11 and 12 of *Schillers sämtliche Werke*, Säkular-Ausgabe, edited by Erich van der Hellen. Stuttgart and Berlin: Cotta.

1943 *Lettres sur l'éducation esthétique de l'homme.* Collection Bilingue des Classiques Etrangers. Edited and translated by Robert Leroux. Paris: Montaigne.

1957 *Über naive und sentimentalische Dichtung.* Edited with an introduction by William F. Mainland. Oxford: Blackwell.

1958 *Schillers Briefe 1794–1795.* Edited by Günter Schulz. Volume 27 of *Schiller's Werke*, Nationalausgabe. Edited by Julius Petersen and others. Weimar: Böhlau.

1959 *Erzählungen. Theoretische Schriften.* Edited by Gerhard Fricke and Herbert Göpfert. Volume 5 of *Schillers sämtliche Werke.* Munich: Hanser.

1962–63 *Philosophische Schriften.* Edited by Benno von Wiese, assisted by Helmut Koopmann. Volumes 20 and 21 of *Schillers Werke*, Nationalausgabe. Ed. by Julius Petersen and others. Weimar: Böhlau.

1966 *Naive and Sentimental Poetry, On the Sublime.* Translated by Julius A. Elias. New York: Ungar.

1967 *On The Aesthetic Education of Man In a Series of Letters: English and German Facing. Edited and Translated with an Introduction, Commentary, and Glossary of Terms* by Elizabeth M. Wilkinson and Leonard A. Willoughby. Oxford: Oxford University Press.

1970 *Vom Pathetischen und Erhabenen: Ausgewählte Schriften zur Dramentheorie.* Edited by Klaus L. Berghahn. Stuttgart: Reclam.

1971 *Kallias oder über die Schönheit: Über Anmut und Würde.* Edited by Klaus L. Berghahn. Stuttgart: Reclam.

1981 *Über die ästhetische Erziehung des Menschen in einer Reihe von Briefen: Text, Materialien, Kommentar.* Edited by Wolfgang Düsing. Munich and Vienna: Hanser.

1981 *On the Naive and Sentimental in Literature.* Translated with an introduction by Helen Watanabe O'Kelly. Manchester: Carcanet.

1985 *On Naive and Sentimental Poetry.* In *German Aesthetic and Literary Criticism: Winckelmann, Lessing, Hamann, Herder, Schiller, Goethe.* Edited by Hugh B. Nisbet. Cambridge: Cambridge University Press.

1992 *Theoretische Schriften.* Edited by Rolf-Peter Janz. Volume 8 of *Friedrich Schiller: Werke und Briefe.* Frankfurt am Main: Deutscher Klassiker Verlag.

Secondary literature

Nicolai, Friedrich. 1796. *Beschreibung einer Reise durch Deutschland und die Schweiz im Jahre 1781: Nebst Bemerkungen über Gelehrsamkeit, Industrie, Religion und Sitten.* Volume 11. Berlin and Stettin.

Schlegel, August Wilhelm. 1802–03. *Vorlesungen über schöne Litteratur und Kunst.* 3 parts in 2 volumes. Heilbronn: Henninger 1884. Volume 2. *Geschichte der klassischen Literatur.*

Richter, Johann Paul (Jean Paul). 1804. *Vorschule der Ästhetik.* 3 volumes. Hamburg: Perthes.

Fülleborn, Georg Gustav. 1801. *Friedrich Schiller: Nebst einigen Fragmenten über ihn.* Breslau: Schall.

Bouterwek, Friedrich. 1819. *Geschichte der deutschen Poesie und Beredsamkeit seit dem Ende des dreizehnten Jahrhunderts,* volume 11. Göttingen: Röwer.

Carlyle, Thomas. 1825. *The Life of Friedrich Schiller: Comprehending an Examination of his Works.* London: Taylor and Hessey.

Menzel, Wolfgang. 1828. *Die deutsche Literatur.* Stuttgart: Franckh.

Humboldt, Wilhelm von. 1830. "Über Schiller und den Gang seiner Geistesentwicklung". In *Briefwechsel zwischen Friedrich von Schiller und Wilhelm von Humboldt.* Stuttgart and Tübingen: Cotta.

Wienbarg, Ludolf. 1834. *Ästhetische Feldzüge: Dem jungen Deutschland gewidmet.* Hamburg: Hoffmann und Campe.

Hegel, Georg Wilhelm Friedrich. 1835–38. *Vorlesungen über die Ästhetik.* 2 volumes. Edited by H.G. Hotho. Berlin: Duncker und Humblot. Republished, Berlin: Aufbau, 1955.

Eckermann, Johann Peter. 1836. *Gespräche mit Goethe in den letzten Jahren seines Lebens.* Leipzig: Brockhaus. Republished and cited here in volume 19 of Goethe. *Sämtliche Werke nach Epochen seines Schaffens.* Munich: Hanser, 1986.

Heine, Heinrich. 1835. *Zur Geschichte der Religion und Philosophie in Deutschland.* Hamburg: Hoffmann und Campe.

Hoffmeister, Karl. 1838–42. *Schiller's Leben, Geistesentwickelung und Werke im Zusammenhang.* 3 volumes. Stuttgart: Balz.

Laube, Heinrich. 1839–40. *Geschichte der deutschen Literatur.* 4 volumes. Stuttgart: Hallberg.

Echtermeyer, Theodor and Arnold Ruge. 1839–40. *Der Protestantismus und die Romantik. Zur Verständigung über die Zeit und ihre Gegensätze. Ein Manifest. Hallische Jahrbücher für deutsche Wissenschaft und Kunst* nos 245–51; 265–71; 301–10 (1839); 53–56; 63–64 (1840). Leipzig: Wigand.

Grün, Karl. 1844. *Friedrich Schiller als Mensch, Geschichtsschreiber, Denker und Dichter: Ein gedrängter Kommentar zu Schiller's sämmtlichen Werken.* Leipzig: Brockhaus.

Danzel, Theodor. 1848. *Schillers Briefwechsel mit Körner.* In *Wiener Jahrbücher der Literatur*, 121: 1–25. Republished also in his *Gesammelte Aufsätze*, edited by Otto Jahn. Leipzig: Dyk. 1855: 227–44.

Gervinus, Georg Gottfried. 1853. *Geschichte der deutschen Dichtung.* 5 volumes. Leipzig: Engelmann.

Hemsen, Wilhelm. 1854. *Schiller's Ansichten über Schönheit und Kunst.* Göttingen: University of Göttingen.

Tomaschek, Karl. 1857. *Schiller und Kant.* Vienna: Tendler.

Fischer, Kuno. 1858. *Schiller als Philosoph.* Frankfurt am Main: Hermann.

Tomaschek, Karl. 1862. *Schiller in seinem Verhältnisse zur Wissenschaft.* Vienna: Gerold.

Müller, Hermann Friedrich. 1876. "Plotin und Schiller über die Schönheit." *Philosophische Monatshefte* 12: 385–93.

Sime, James. 1882. *Schiller.* Foreign Classics for English Readers. Edinburgh: Blackwood.

Überweg, Friedrich. 1884. *Schiller als Historiker und Philosoph.* Leipzig: Reissner.

Schlegel, Friedrich. 1890. *Briefe an seinen Bruder August Wilhelm*. Edited by Oskar Walzel. Berlin: Speyer und Peters.

Bosanquet, Bernard. 1892. *A History of Aesthetic*. London: Sonnenschein.

Harnack, Otto. 1892. *Die klassische Ästhetik der Deutschen: Würdigung der kunsttheoretischen Arbeiten Schiller's Goethe's und ihrer Freunde*. Leipzig: Hinrich.

Sommer, Robert. 1892. *Grundzüge einer Geschichte der deutschen Psychologie und Ästhetik von Wolff-Baumgarten bis Kant-Schiller*. Würzburg: Stahel. Reprinted, Hildesheim and New York: Olms, 1975.

Gneisse, Karl. 1893. *Schillers Lehre von der ästhetischen Wahrnehmung*. Berlin: Weidmann.

Berger, Karl. 1894. *Die Entwicklung von Schillers Ästhetik*. Weimar: Böhlau.

Vorländer, Karl. 1894. "Ethischer Rigorismus und sittliche Schönheit. Mit besonderer Berücksichtigung von Kant und Schiller." *Philosophische Monatshefte* 30, nos 5–6: 225–405, 9–10: 534–77.

Kühnemann, Eugen. 1895. *Kants und Schillers Begründung der Ästhetik*. Munich: Beck.

Vorländer, Karl. 1898. "Kant — Schiller — Goethe. Eine Apologie." *Kantstudien* 3: 130–41.

Gaede, Udo. 1899. *Schillers Abhandlung "Über naive und sentimentalische Dichtung." Studien zur Entstehungsgeschichte*. Berlin: Duncker und Humblot.

Basch, Victor. 1902. *La Poétique de Schiller*. Paris: Alcan.

Thomas, Calvin. 1902. *The Life and Works of Schiller*. New York: Holt.

Bauch, Bruno. 1903. "*Naiv* und *Sentimentalisch* — *Klassisch* und *Romantisch*." *Archiv für Geschichte der Philosophie* 9: 486–515.

Saintsbury, George. 1904. *A History of Criticism and Literary Taste in Europe from the Earliest Texts to the Present Day*. Volume 3. Edinburgh and London: Blackwood.

Mehring, Franz. 1905. *Schiller: Ein Lebensbild für deutsche Arbeiter*. Leipzig: Leipziger Buchdruckerei.

Robertson, James G. 1905. *Schiller after a Century*. Edinburgh and London: Blackwood.

Windelband, Wilhelm. 1905. "Schillers transcendentaler Idealismus." *Kantstudien* 10: 398–411.

Vorländer, Karl. 1907. *Kant — Goethe — Schiller: Gesammelte Aufsätze*. Leipzig: Dürr.

Engel, Bernhard Carl. 1908. *Schiller als Denker: Prologomena zu Schillers philosophischen Schriften*. Berlin: Weidmann.

Wilm, Emil Carl. 1908. "The Kantian Studies of Schiller." *Journal of English and Germanic Philology* 7: 126–33.

Wilm, Emil Carl. 1910. "The Relation of Schiller to Post-Kantian Idealism." *Journal of English and Germanic Philology* 9: 20–24.

Mugdan, Bertha. 1911. *Die theoretischen Grundlagen der Schillerschen Philosophie*. *Kantstudien*, Ergänzungsheft im Auftrag der Kantgesellschaft, no. 19. Berlin: Renther und Reichard.

Ludwig, Albert. 1911. *Schiller und die deutsche Nachwelt*. Berlin: Weidmann.

Rosalewski, Willy. 1912. *Schillers Ästhetik im Verhältnis zur Kantischen*. Heidelberg: Winter.

Carritt, Edgar F. 1914. *The Theory of Beauty*. London: Methuen.

Müller, Hermann Friedrich. 1915. "Plotinos über ästhetische Erziehung." *Neue Jahrbücher für das klassische Altertum* 36: 69–79.

Cassirer, Ernst. 1916. *Freiheit und Form: Studien zur deutschen Geistesgeschichte*. Berlin: Bruno Cassirer. Reprinted, Darmstadt: Wissenschaftliche Buchgesellschaft, 1961.

Lovejoy, Arthur O. 1920. 'Schiller and the Genesis of German Romanticism'. *Modern Language Notes* 35: 1–9 (Part 1); 136–46 (Part 2).

Cassirer, Ernst. 1921. *Idee und Gestalt: Goethe — Schiller — Hölderlin — Kleist*. Berlin: Bruno Cassirer.

Jung, Carl Gustav. 1921. *Psychologische Typen*. Zurich: Rascher. Translated by H. G. Baynes as *Psychological Types*. London: Paul, Trench and Trubner and New York: Harcourt, Brace.

Babbitt, Irving. 1922. "Schiller and Romanticism." *Modern Language Notes* 37: 257–68.

Lovejoy, Arthur O. 1922. "Reply to Professor Babbitt." *Modern Language Notes* 37: 268–74

Koch, Franz. 1926. *Schillers philosophische Schriften und Plotin*. Leipzig: Weber.

Schmeer, Hans. 1926. *Der Begriff der "schönen Seele" besonders bei Wieland und in der deutschen Literatur des 18. Jahrhunderts*. Berlin: Ebering. Reprinted, Nendeln: Kraus, 1967.

Böhm, Wilhelm. 1927. *Schillers "Briefe über die ästhetische Erziehung"*. Halle an der Saale: Niemeyer.

Korff, Hermann A. 1927. *Geist der Goethezeit: Versuch einer ideellen Entwicklung der klassisch-romantischen Literaturgeschichte*. Part 2.

Kommerell, Max. 1928. *Der Dichter als Führer in der deutschen Klassik*. Berlin: Bondi.

Lutz, Hans. 1928. *Schillers Anschauungen von Kultur und Natur*. Berlin: Ebering.

Meyer, Theodor M. 1928. 'Der Griechentraum Schillers und seine philosophische Begründung.' *Jahrbuch des Freien Deutschen Hochstifts*: 125–53.

Babbitt, Irving. 1932. "Schiller as Aesthetic Theorist." In his *On Being Creative*. Cambridge, Mass.: Harvard University Press: 134–86.

Basch, Victor. 1934. "Le Kallias de Schiller". In *Mélanges Henri Lichtenberger*. Paris: Librairie Stock: 99–121.

Cysarz, Herbert. 1934. *Schiller*. Halle: Niemeyer.

Butler, Eliza M. 1935. *The Tyranny of Greece over Germany: A Study of the Influence Exercised by Greek Art and Poetry over the Great German Writers of the Eighteenth, Nineteenth and Twentieth Centuries*. Cambridge: Cambridge University Press.

Cassirer, Ernst. 1935. "Schiller and Shaftesbury." *Publications of the English Goethe Society* 11: 37–59.

Deubel, Werner. 1935. *Schillers Kampf um die Tragödie: Umrisse eines neuen Schillerbildes*. Berlin-Lichterfelde: Widerkind.

Lovejoy, Arthur O. 1936. *The Great Chain of Being*. Cambridge, Mass.: Harvard University Press.

Meng, Heinrich. 1936. *Schillers Abhandlung über naive und sentimentalische Dichtung. Prologomena zu einer Typologie des Dichterischen*. Frauenfeld and Leipzig: Huber.

Rehm, Walter. 1936. *Griechentum und Goethezeit*. Leipzig: Dietrich.

Baumecker, Gottfried. 1937. *Schillers Schönheitslehre*. Heidelberg: Winter.

Buchwald, Reinhard. 1937. *Schiller*. 2 vols. Leipzig: Insel.

Leroux, Robert. 1937. "Schiller, théoricien de l'état." *Revue Germanique*: 1–28.

Viëtor, Karl. 1937. "Die Idee des Erhabenen in der deutschen Literatur." In *Harvard Studies and Notes in Philology and Literature*, volume 19. Cambridge, Mass.: Harvard University Press. Revised and enlarged in his *Geist und Form. Aufsätze zur deutschen Literatur*. Berne: Francke, 1952: 234–66.

Stahl, Ernst L. 1938. "The Genesis of Schiller's Theory of Tragedy". In *German Studies Presented to H.G. Fiedler*. Oxford: Oxford University Press: 403–23.

Spranger, Eduard. 1941. *Schillers Geistesart gespiegelt in seinen philosophischen Schriften und Gedichten.* Abhandlungen der Preussischen Akademie der Wissenschaften. Berlin: Akademie der Wissenschaften.

Read, Herbert. 1943. *Education through Art.* London: Faber.

Cassirer, Ernst. 1944. *An Essay on Man.* New Haven, Conn.: Yale University Press.

Lukács, Georg. 1947. "Schillers Theorie der modernen Literatur." In *Goethe und seine Zeit.* Bern: Francke: 78–109. Translated by Robert Anchor as "Schiller's Theory of Modern Literature." In *Goethe and His Age.* London: Anchor. 1968: 101–35.

Bohning, Elizabeth. 1949. "Goethe's and Schiller's Interpretation of Beauty." *German Quarterly* 22: 185–94.

Witte, William. 1949. *Schiller.* Oxford: Blackwell.

Gerhard, Melitta. 1950. *Schiller.* Bern: Francke.

Reiner, Hans. 1951 *Pflicht und Neigung: Die Grundlagen der Sittlichkeit, erörtert und neu bestimmt mit besonderm Bezug auf Kant und Schiller.* Mersenheim am Glan: Hain. Second edition 1954. Translated by Mark Santos as *Duty and Inclination. The Fundamentals of Morality Discussed and Defined with Special Regard to Kant and Schiller.* The Hague: Nijhoff. 1983.

Schütz, Oskar. 1951. *Schillers Theorie des Schönen.* Schlehdorf: Bronnen.

Abrams, Meyer H. 1953. *The Mirror and the Lamp: Romantic Theory and the Critical Tradition.* Oxford and New York: Oxford University Press.

Langer, Susanne K. 1953. *Feeling and Form. A Theory of Art Developed from Philosophy in a New Key.* London: Routledge and Kegan Paul.

Popitz, Heinrich. 1953. *Der entfremdete Mensch: Zeitkritik und Geschichtsphilosophie des jungen Marx.* Philosophische Forschung. Neue Folge. Basel: Verlag für Recht und Gesellschaft.

Lukács, Georg. 1954. "Zur Ästhetik Schillers." In his *Beiträge zur Geschichte der Ästhetik.* Berlin: Aufbau: 11–96.

Stahl, Ernst L. 1954. *Friedrich Schiller's Drama: Theory and Practice.* Oxford: Oxford University Press.

Willoughby, Leonard A. 1954. "Schiller on Man's Education to Freedom through Knowledge." *Germanic Review* 29: 163–74.

Abusch, Alexander. 1955. "Die Briefe über die ästhetische Erziehung des Menschen." In *Schiller in unserer Zeit: Beiträge zum Schillerjahr 1955.* Weimar: Volksverlag: 95–102.

Eichner, Hans. 1955. "The Supposed Influence of Schiller's *Über naive und sentimentalische Dichtung* on F. Schlegel's *Über das Studium der griechischen Poesie.*" *Germanic Review* 30 (1955): 260–64.

Marcuse, Herbert. 1955. *Eros and Civilization: A Philosophical Enquiry into Freud.* Boston: Beacon Press.

Wellek, René. 1955. *A History of Modern Criticism 1750–1950.* Volume 1: *The Later Eighteenth Century.* London: Cape.

Wilkinson, Elizabeth M. 1955. "Schiller's Concept of *Schein* in the Light of Recent Aesthetics." *German Quarterly* 28: 219–27.

Hamburger, Käte. 1956. "Schillers Fragment 'Der Menschenfeind' und die Idee der Kalokagathie." *Deutsche Vierteljahrsschrift* 30: 367–400.

Reiss, Hans S. 1956–57. "The Concept of the Aesthetic State in the Work of Schiller and Novalis." *Publications of the English Goethe Society* 26: 26–51.

Fambach, Oscar. 1957. *Ein Jahrhundert deutscher Literaturkritik (1750–1850).* Volume 2: *Schiller und sein Kreis in der Kritik ihrer Zeit.* Berlin: Akademie

Henrich, Dieter. 1957. "Der Begriff der Schönheit in Schillers Ästhetik." *Zeitschrift für philosophische Forschung* 11: 527–47. Translated as "Beauty and Freedom. Schiller's Struggle with Kant's Aesthetics." In *Essays in Kant's Aesthetics.* Edited by Ted Cohen and Paul Guyer. Chicago and London: University of Chicago Press, 1982: 236–57.

Bock, Erwin. 1958. "Über das Verhältnis von Ethik und Ästhetik in Schillers philosophischen Schriften." Dissertation, University of Leipzig.

Brinkmann, Richard. 1958. "Romantische Dichtungstheorien in Friedrich Schlegels Frühschriften und Schillers Begriff des Naiven und Sentimentalischen. Vorzeichen einer Emanzipation des Historischen." *Deutsche Vierteljahrsschrift* 32: 344–71.

Boucher, Maurice. 1959. "Le 'Sauvage' et le 'Barbare' dans les *Lettres sur L'Education esthétique.*" *Etudes Germaniques* 14: 333–37.

David, Claude. 1959. "La Notion de 'Nature' chez Schiller." *Publications of the English Goethe Society* 29: 1–25

Hamburger, Käte. 1959. "Schiller und Sarte. Ein Versuch zum Idealismus-Problem Schillers." *Jahrbuch der Deutschen Schillergesellschaft* 3: 34–70.

Hatfield, Henry. 1959. "Schiller, Winckelmann and the Myth of Greece." In *Friedrich Schiller 1759/1959: Commemorative American Studies.* Edited by John R. Frey. Urbana: University of Illinois Press: 12–25.

Jaeger, Hans. 1959. "Schillers Philosophie der Existenz." In *Schiller 1759/1959. Commemorative American Studies.* Edited by John R. Frey. Urbana: University of Illinois Press: 36–57.

Meyer, Herman. 1959. "Schillers philosophische Rhetorik." *Euphorion* 53: 313–50.

Miller, Ronald D. 1959. *Schiller and the Ideal of Freedom: A Study of Schiller's Philosophical Works with Chapters on Kant*. Harrogate: Duchy Press. Reprinted, Oxford University Press, 1970.

Müller, Joachim. 1959. *Das Edle in der Freiheit: Schillerstudien*. Leipzig: Koehler und Amelang.

Rohrmoser, Günter. 1959. "Zum Problem der ästhetischen Versöhnung. Schiller und Hegel." *Euphorion* 53: 351–66.

Seidel, Siegfried. 1959. "Die Überwindung des subjektiven Idealismus bei Schiller." *Weimarer Beiträge* 5, Sonderheft: 149–79.

Träger, Claus. 1959. 'Schiller als Theoretiker des Übergangs vom Ideal zur Wirklichkeit.' *Sinn und Form* 11: 546–76. Republished as prefatory essay to *Friedrich Schiller: Über Kunst und Wirklichkeit. Schriften und Briefe zur Ästhetik*. Edited by Claus Träger. Leipzig: Reclam, 1959. Third edition, 1984.

Wiese, Benno von. 1959. *Schiller*. Stuttgart: Metzler.

Witte, William. 1959. "Law and the Social Order in Schiller's Thought." In his *Schiller and Burns and Other Essays*. Oxford: Blackwell: 67–80

Binder, Wolfgang. 1960. "Die Begriffe 'naiv' und 'sentimentalisch' und Schillers Drama." *Jahrbuch der Deutschen Schillergesellschaft* 4: 140–57.

Mann, Thomas. 1960. "Goethe und Tolstoi." In *Reden und Aufsätze* 1. Volume 9 of *Gesammelte Werke in zwölf Bänden*. Frankfurt am Main: Fischer: 58–173.

Read, Herbert. 1960. *The Third Realm of Education: The Burton Lecture*. Cambridge, Mass.: Harvard University Press.

Wilkinson, Elizabeth M. 1960. "Reflections after Translating Schiller's *Letters on the Aesthetic Education of Man*." *Schiller: Bicentenary Lectures*. Edited by F. Norman. London: University of London, Institute of Germanic Studies: 46–82.

Wilkinson, Elizabeth M. 1960. "Schiller und die Idee der Aufklärung. Betrachtungen anläßlich der Briefe über die ästhetische Erziehung." *Jahrbuch der Deutschen Schillergesellschaft* 4: 42–59

Kerry, Stanley S. 1961. *Schiller's Writings on Aesthetics*. Manchester: Manchester University Press.

Latzel, Sigbert. 1961. "Die ästhetische Vernunft. Bemerkungen zu Schillers 'Kallias' mit Bezug auf die Ästhetik des 18. Jahrhunderts." *Literaturwissenschaftliches Jahrbuch*, Neue Folge 2: 31–40.

Lohner, Edgar. 1961. "Schillers Begriff des Scheins und die moderne Lyrik." *Deutsche Beiträge zur geistigen Überlieferung* 4: 131–81.

Wilkinson, Elizabeth M. 1961. *Schiller — Poet or Philosopher?*. Oxford: Oxford University Press.

Gadamer, Hans-Georg. 1962. *Wahrheit und Methode: Grundzüge einer philosophischen Hermeneutik*. Tübingen: Mohr. Translated as *Truth and Method*. London: Sheed and Ward, 1975.

Pascal, Roy. 1962. " 'Bildung' and the Division of Labour." In *German Studies Presented to W.H. Bruford*. London, Toronto, Wellington and Sydney: Harrap: 14–28.

Sayce, Olive. 1962. "Das Problem der Vieldeutigkeit in Schillers ästhetischer Terminologie." *Jahrbuch der Deutschen Schillergesellschaft* 6: 149–77.

Burger, Heinz Otto. 1963. "Europäisches Adelsideal und Deutsche Klassik." In his *Dasein heißt eine Rolle spielen: Studien zur deutschen Literaturgeschichte*. Munich: Hanser: 211–32.

Wiese, Benno von. 1963. "Die Utopie des Ästhetischen bei Schiller." In *Zwischen Utopie und Wirklichkeit. Studien zur deutschen Literatur*. Düsseldorf: Bagel: 81–101.

Hatfield, H. 1964. *Aesthetic Paganism in German Literature from Winckelmann to the Death of Goethe*. Cambridge, MA: Harvard University Press.

Hermand, Jost. 1964. "Schillers Abhandlung 'Über naive und sentimentalische Dichtung' im Lichte der deutschen Popularphilosophie des 18. Jahrhunderts." *PMLA* 79: 428–41.

Ives, Margaret C. 1964. "Musical Elements in Schiller's Concept of Harmony". *German Life and Letters* 18: 111–16.

Schaper, Eva. 1964: "Friedrich Schiller: Adventures of a Kantian." *British Journal of Aesthetics* 4: 438–62

Wilkinson, Elizabeth M. 1964. "Schiller and the Gutenberg Galaxy: A Question of Appropriate Contexts." *German Life and Letters* 18: 309–18.

Wells, George A. 1966. "Schiller's View of Nature in *Über naive und sentimentalische Dichtung*." *Journal of English and Germanic Philology* 65: 491–510.

Calder, William M. 1967. "Schiller on the Will and on the Heroic Villain." *Oxford German Studies* 2: 41–54

Düsing, Wolfgang. 1967. *Schillers Idee des Erhabenen*. Cologne: Gonder & Hansen.

Jauss, Hans Robert. 1967. "Fr. Schlegels und Fr. Schillers Replik auf die 'Querelle des Anciens et des Modernes.' " In *Europäische Aufklärung: Herbert Dieckmann zum 60. Geburtstag.* Edited by Hugo Friedrich and Fritz Schalk. Munich: Fink: 117–40.

Oellers, Norbert. 1967. *Schiller: Geschichte seiner Wirkung bis zu Goethes Tod 1805–1832.* Bonn: Bouvier.

Ellis, John M. 1969. *Schiller's "Kalliasbriefe" and the Study of His Aesthetic Theory.* The Hague and Paris: Mouton.

Wilkinson, Elizabeth M. and Leonard A. Willoughby. 1969. " 'The Whole Man' in Schiller's Theory of Culture and Society. On the Virtue of a Plurality of Models." *Essays in German Language, Culture and Society.* Edited by Siegbert Prawer and others. London: University of London, Institute of Germanic Studies: 177–210.

Heuer, Fritz. 1970. *Darstellung der Freiheit. Schillers transzendentale Frage nach der Kunst.* Cologne and Vienna: Böhlau.

Ives, Margaret C. 1970. *The Analogue of Harmony: Some Reflections on Schiller's Philosophical Essays.* Duquesne Studies Philological Series, no. 13. Pittsburgh: Duquesne University Press.

Oellers, Norbert (ed.) 1970. *Schiller - Zeitgenosse aller Epochen. Dokumente zur Wirkungsgeschichte Schillers in Deutschland.* 2 vols. Vol. 1 Frankfurt am Main: Athenäum. Vol. 2 Munich: Beck, 1976.

Abrams, Meyer H. 1971. *Natural Supernaturalism. Tradition and Revolution in Romantic Literature.* New York and London: Norton.

Berghahn, Klaus L. 1971. " 'Das Pathetischerhabene': Schillers Dramentheorie." In *Deutsche Dramentheorien.* Edited by Reinhold Grimm. Frankfurt am Main: Athenäum: 214–44.

Hinderer, Walter. 1971. "Zwischen Person und Existenz: Vergleichende Bemerkungen zu Schillers philosophischer Anthropologie." *Germanisch-Romanische Monatsschrift.* 52: 257–68.

Jameson, Frederic. 1971. *Marxism and Form.* Princeton: Princeton University Press.

Sautermeister, Gerd. 1971. *Idyllik und Dramatik im Werk Friedrich Schillers. Zum geschichtlichen Ort seiner klassischen Dramen.* Stuttgart and Berlin: Kohlhammer.

Ueding, Gerd. 1971. *Schillers Rhetorik: Idealistische Wirkungsästhetik und rhetorische Tradition.* Tübingen: Niemeyer.

Wessell, Leonard P. 1971. "Schiller and the Genesis of German Romanticism." *Studies in Romanticism* 10: 175–98.

Barnouw, Jeffrey. 1972. " 'Der Trieb, bestimmt zu werden'. Herder, Schiller und Schelling als Antwort auf Fichte." *Deutsche Vierteljahrsschrift* 46: 248–93.

Szondi, Peter. 1972. "Das Naive ist das Sentimentalische: Zur Begriffsdialektik in Schillers Abhandlung *Über naive und sentimentalische Dichtung.*" *Euphorion* 66: 174–206.

Borchmeyer, Dieter. 1973. *Tragödie und Öffentlichkeit. Schillers Dramaturgie im Zusammenhang seiner ästhetisch-politischen Theorie und die rhetorische Tradition.* Munich: Fink.

Janz, Rolf-Peter. 1973. *Autonomie und soziale Funktion der Kunst: Studien zur Ästhetik von Schiller und Novalis.* Stuttgart: Metzler.

Bürger, Peter. 1974. *Theorie der Avantgarde.* Frankfurt am Main: Suhrkamp.

Pfeifer, Eleonora. 1974. Die Aufhebung kulturphilosophischer und ästhetisch-theoretischer Leistungen Friedrich Schillers in der marxistisch-leninistischer Kulturtheorie und Ästhetik. Dissertation, Karl-Marx-Universität Leipzig.

Düsing, Wolfgang. 1975. "Ästhetische Form als Darstellung der Subjektivität." In *Friedrich Schiller. Zur Geschichtlichkeit seines Werkes.* Kronberg im Taunus: Scriptor: 197–239.

Pfeifer, Eleonora. 1976. "Die Kulturauffassung Friedrich Schillers in kulturtheoretischer Sicht." *Weimarer Beiträge* 22: 87–111.

Delinière, Jean. 1977. L'image de Schiller dans la critique littéraire allemande de 1832 à 1859. Dissertation University of Paris-Sorbonne.

Janke, Wolfgang. 1977. *Historische Dialektik: Destruktion dialektischer Grundformen von Kant bis Marx.* Berlin and New York: de Gruyter.

Kaiser, Gerhard. 1977. *Wandrer und Idylle: Goethe und die Phänomenologie der Natur in der deutschen Dichtung von Gessner bis Gottfried Keller.* Göttingen: Vandenhoeck und Ruprecht.

Mettler, Heinrich. 1977. *Entfremdung und Revolution: Brennpunkt des Klassischen. Studien zu Schillers Briefen "Über die ästhetische Erziehung des Menschen" im Hinblick auf die Begegnung mit Goethe.* Bern and Munich: Francke.

Strube, Werner. 1977. "Schillers Kallias-Briefe oder über die Objektivität der Schönheit." *Literaturwissenschaftliches Jahrbuch* 18: 115–31.

Dewhurst, Kenneth and Nigel Reeves. 1978. *Friedrich Schiller: Medicine, Psychology and Literature.* Oxford: Sandford.

Ewers, Hans-Harro. 1978. *Die schöne Individualität: Zur Genesis des bürgerlichen Kunstideals.* Stuttgart: Metzler.

Schaper, Eva. 1979. "Schiller's Kant: A Chapter in the History of a Creative Misunderstanding." In her *Studies in Kant's Aesthetics*. Edinburgh: Edinburgh University Press: 99–115.

Ashton, Rosemary. 1980. *The German Idea: Four English Writers and the Reception of German Thought 1800–1860*. Cambridge: Cambridge University Press.

Barnouw, Jeffrey. 1980. "The Morality of the Sublime: Kant and Schiller." *Studies in Romanticism* 19, no. 4: 497–514.

Holmes, Terry. 1980. "Property and Politics in Schiller's Theory of Aesthetic Education." *Oxford German Studies* 11: 27–39.

Pott, Hans-Georg. 1980. *Die schöne Freiheit: Eine Interpretation zu Schillers Schrift "Über die ästhetische Erziehung des Menschen."* Munich: Fink.

Schings, Hans-Jürgen. 1980. *Der mitleidigste Mensch ist der beste Mensch. Poetik des Mitleids von Lessing bis Büchner*. Munich: Beck.

Rippere, Victoria. 1981. *Schiller and "Alienation."* Bern, Frankfurt am Main, and Las Vegas: Lang.

Barnouw, Jeffrey. 1982. " 'Freiheit zu geben durch Freiheit': Ästhetischer Zustand — Ästhetischer Staat." In *Friedrich Schiller. Kunst, Humanität und Politik in der späten Aufklärung. Ein Symposium*. Edited by Wolfgang Wittkowski. Tübingen: Niemeyer: 138–63.

Doppler, Alfred. 1982. "Geschichtliche Situation und ästhetische Konzeption. Bemerkungen zu Schillers Briefen 'Über die ästhetische Erziehung des Menschen.' " In *Tradition und Entwicklung: Festschrift Eugen Thurnher zum 60. Geburtstag*. Edited by Werner Bauer. Innsbruck: Innsbruck University.

Hinderer, Walter. 1982. "Utopische Elemente in Schillers ästhetischer Anthropologie." In *Literarische Utopie-Entwürfe*. Edited by Hiltrud Gnüg. Frankfurt am Main: Suhrkamp: 173–86.

Kain, Philip J. 1982. *Schiller, Hegel and Marx: State, Society and the Aesthetic Ideal of Ancient Greece*. Kingston and Montreal: McGill-Queen's University Press.

Wessell, Leonard P. 1982. *The Philosophical Background to Friedrich Schiller's Aesthetics of Living Form*. Frankfurt am Main and Bern: Lang.

Borchmeyer, Dieter. 1983. "Rhetorische und ästhetische Revolutionskritik: Edmund Burke und Schiller." In *Klassik und Moderne: Die Weimarer Klassik als historisches Ereignis und Herausforderung im kulturgeschichtlichen Prozeß*. Edited by Karl Richter and Jörg Schönert. Stuttgart: Metzler: 56–79.

Borchmeyer, Dieter. 1984. "Aufklärung und praktische Kultur. Schillers Idee der ästhetischen Erziehung." In *Naturplan und Verfallskritik: Zu Begriff und Geschichte der Kultur*. Edited by Helmut Brackert and Fritz Wefelmeyer. Frankfurt am Main: Suhrkamp.

Man, Paul de. 1984. "Aesthetic Formalization: Kleist's *Über das Marionettentheater*." In his *The Rhetoric of Romanticism*. New York: Columbia University Press: 263–90.

Habermas, Jürgen. 1985. *Der philosophische Diskurs der Moderne. Zwölf Vorlesungen*. Frankfurt am Main: Suhrkamp.

Kim Kwang-Myung. 1985. *"Die vollständige anthropologische Schätzung" bei Schiller in ihrer Bedeutung für seine Ästhetik - eine Interpretation zu Schillers philosophisch-ästhetischen Schriften*. Würzburg: University of Würzburg.

Meier, Albert. 1985. "Der Grieche, die Natur und die Geschichte." *Jahrbuch der Deutschen Schillergesellschaft* 29: 113–24.

Marx, Wolfgang. 1986. "Schillers 'sentimentalische' Philosophie und ihre 'naiven' Komponenten." *Jahrbuch der Deutschen Schillergesellschaft*. 30: 251–65.

Disselbeck, Klaus. 1987. *Geschmack und Kunst: Eine systemtheoretische Untersuchung zu Schillers Briefen "Über die ästhetische Erziehung des Menschen"*. Opladen: Westdeutscher Verlag.

Kontje, Todd C. 1987. *Constructing Reality: A Rhetorical Analysis of Friedrich Schiller's Letters on the Aesthetic Education of Man*. New York, Bern, and Frankfurt am Main: Lang.

Savile, Anthony. 1987. *Aesthetic Reconstructions: The Seminal Writings of Lessing, Kant and Schiller*. Aristotelian Society Series, volume 8. Oxford: Blackwell: 195–254.

Tschierske, Ulrich. 1988. *Vernunftkritik und ästhetische Subjektivität: Studien zur Anthropologie Friedrich Schillers*. Tübingen: Niemeyer.

Borchmeyer, Dieter. 1989. "Kritik der Aufklärung im Geist der Aufklärung." In *Aufklärung und Gegenaufklärung in der europäischen Literatur, Philosophie und Politik von der Antike bis zur Gegenwart*. Edited by Jochen Schmidt. Darmstadt: Wissenschaftliche Buchgesellschaft: 361–76.

Chytry, Josef. 1989. *The Aesthetic State: A Quest in Modern German Thought*. Berkeley, Los Angeles, and London: University of California Press.

Muehleck-Müller, Cathleen. 1989. *Schönheit und Freiheit: Die Vollendung der Moderne in der Kunst. Schiller — Kant*. Epistemata: Würzburger wissenschaftliche Schriften Reihe Literaturwissenschaft no. 36. Würzburg: Königshausen und Neumann.

Eagleton, Terry. 1990. *The Ideology of the Aesthetic*. Oxford and Cambridge, Mass.: Blackwell.

Janz, Rolf-Peter. 1990. "Die ästhetische Bewältigung des Schreckens: Zu Schillers Theorie des Erhabenen." In *Geschichte als Literatur: Formen und Grenzen der Repräsentation von Vergangenheit.* Edited by Hartmut Eggert and others. Stuttgart: Metzler: 151–60.

Redfield, Mark. 1990. "De Man, Schiller and the Politics of Reception." *Colloquium Helveticum* 11/12: 139–68.

Pfotenhauer, Helmut. 1991. "Anthropologische Ästhetik und Kritik der ästhetischen Urteilskraft oder Herder, Schiller, die antike Plastik und Seitenblicke auf Kant." In his *Um 1800: Konfigurationen der Literatur, Kunstliteratur und Ästhetik.* Tübingen: Niemeyer: 201–20.

Pugh, David. 1991. "Schiller as Platonist." *Colloquia Germanica* 24: 273–95.

Sharpe, Lesley. 1991. *Friedrich Schiller: Drama, Thought and Politics.* Cambridge: Cambridge University Press.

Hansen, Frank-Peter. 1992. "Die Rezeption von Kants *Kritik der Urteilskraft* in Schillers Briefen *Über die ästhetische Erziehung des Menschen.*" *Literaturwissenschaftliches Jahrbuch* 33: 167–88.

Fischer, Bernd. 1994. "Goethes Klassizismus und Schillers Poetologie der Moderne: *Über naive und sentimentalische Dichtung.*" *Zeitschrift für deutsche Philologie* 113: 225–45.

Index

Schiller's individual works are listed under the index entry for Schiller. The exception is the *Ästhetische Briefe*, a work mentioned on almost every page of this book. Key concepts in that work (for example, Aesthetic State, Schein) are listed alphabetically here.

Abrams, Meyer H. 35, 53, 65–66, 109, 124, 128
Abusch, Alexander 87, 88, 124
Adorno, Theodor W. 75, 89, 90
Aesthetic State 4, 32, 35, 48, 56, 59, 66, 86, 90, 91, 93, 94–101, 106
Aristotle 4, 23, 34, 67, 106
Ashton, Rosemary 35, 130

Babbitt, Irving 51–52, 122, 123
Barnouw, Jeffrey 74, 84–85, 86, 91, 100, 101, 129, 130
Bärwinkel, Roland xi
Basch, Victor 30–31, 39, 55, 121, 123
Bauch, Bruno 30, 121
Baumecker, Gottfried 39, 51, 123
Becher, Johannes R. 87
Berger, Karl 28–29, 121
Berghahn, Klaus L. 73
Binder, Wolfgang 112, 126
Bloch, Ernst 91, 99
Böhm, Wilhelm 46–47, 48, 51, 122
Bohning, Elizabeth 59, 124
Borchmeyer, Dieter 101, 105–106, 129, 130, 131
Bock, Erwin 86, 126
Bosanquet, Bernard 36, 121
Bouterwek, Friedrich 9, 119
Brinkmann, Richard 110, 111, 125
Bruford, Walter H. 91
Buchwald, Reinhard 43, 123
Burger, Heinz O. 104, 127
Bürger, Peter 92, 129
Burke, Edmund 54, 86, 106
Butler, Eliza M. 54, 115, 123

Calder, William F. 72, 79, 127
Carlyle, Thomas 35–36, 119
Cartesian dualism 25

Carritt, Edgar F. 36–37, 122
Cassirer, Ernst 39, 40, 53–54, 56–57, 67, 85, 122, 123, 124
Chytry, Thomas 100–101, 131
Cohen, Hermann 26
Coleridge, Samuel T. 35
Cooper, Anthony Ashley, Lord Shaftesbury 32, 37, 48, 53–54, 59, 60, 69, 77, 85
Cysarz, Herbert 42–43, 123

Danzel, Theodor 18–19, 22, 23, 120
Darwin, Charles 57
David, Claude 70–71, 125
Delinière, Jean 14, 129
Dennis, John 74
Deubel, Werner, 42, 123
Dewhurst, Kenneth 91, 102, 129
Disselbeck, Klaus 100, 131
Doppler, Alfred 99–100, 130
Düsing, Wolfgang 71–72, 82, 119, 127, 129

Eagleton, Terry 84, 93, 131
Eckermann, Johann P. 9, 30, 120
Echtermeyer, Theodor 15, 120
Eichner, Hans 110, 125
Elias, Julius A. 72–73, 108, 118
Ellis, John M. 68–69, 128
Enlightenment, the 15, 24, 58, 74, 87, 100, 101–103, 106, 110
Engel, Bernhard C. 34, 122
Engels, Friedrich 80
Euripides 10
Ewers, Hans-Heino 92, 129

Fambach, Oscar 8, 125
Ferguson, Adam 87, 91

Fichte, Johann G. 8, 9, 23, 36, 37, 40, 51, 85, 91, 102, 104
Fischer, Bernd 115, 132
Fischer, Kuno 20–21, 23, 120
Formtrieb 9, 40, 49, 53, 62, 85, 97, 100
French Revolution, the 4, 41, 56, 60, 63, 65, 83, 87, 89, 96, 97, 99, 102, 105, 106
Freud, Sigmund 90, 114
Fricke, Gerhard 60–61, 118
Fülleborn, Georg G. 9, 119

Gadamer, Hans-Georg 95–96, 127
Gaede, Udo 30, 121
Garve, Christian 9, 111
Geistesgeschichte 39, 40–41
George, Stefan 41, 59, 68
Gerhard, Melitta 59, 124
German Democratic Republic 58, 60, 63, 86, 87, 88, 89, 108, 109
Gervinus, Georg G. 15, 16–17, 18, 120
Gneisse, Karl 25–26, 28, 33, 121
Goedeke, Karl 20, 118
Goethe, Johann W. 5, 8, 9–10, 12, 13, 14, 16, 18, 20, 23–27, 30, 32, 36, 39–41, 43, 44, 49–51, 53, 59, 83, 86, 89, 91, 113, 114, 115
Goebbels, Joseph 84
Göpfert, Herbert 60–61, 118
Graham, Ilse A. 95
Gramsci, Antonio 93, 94
Grün, Karl 15, 16–17, 120

Habermas, Jürgen 93, 105, 131
Hamburger, Käte 63, 77, 78, 79, 82, 125
Hansen, Frank-Peter 84, 132
Harnack, Otto 29, 121
Hatfield, Henry 115, 125, 127
Hegel, Georg W. F. 12–13, 17, 36, 37, 58, 69, 74, 76, 80, 87, 92, 109, 113, 120
Heidegger, Martin 78, 80
Heine, Heinrich 15, 120
Hellen, Erich von der 32, 118
Hemsen, Wilhelm 21–22, 120
Henrich, Dieter 63, 75–76, 125
Herder, Johann G. 11, 17, 24, 25, 31, 32, 36, 49, 50, 65, 84, 86, 115
Hermand, Jost 111, 127

Heuer, Fritz 82, 128
Hinderer, Walter 79–80, 99, 128, 130
Hobbes, Thomas 100
Hoffmeister, Karl 15–16, 17, 120
Holmes, Terry M. 98, 130
Humboldt, Wilhelm von 8, 12, 13–14, 16, 21, 56, 91, 119

Ives, Margaret 69, 127, 128

Jaeger, Hans 79, 125
Jameson, Frederic 91, 114, 128
Janke, Wolfgang 97–98, 129
Janz, Rolf-Peter 66–67, 74–75, 96–97, 119, 129, 132
Jauss, Hans R. 110, 128
Jonas, Fritz 27
Jung, Carl G. xii, 41, 45–46, 122

Kain, Philip J. 99, 130
Kaiser, Gerhard 114, 129
Kant, Immanuel xi, 2, 3, 8, 9, 12, 13, 16, 17, 18, 21, 22, 23, 26, 27, 28, 29, 32, 33, 34, 36, 39, 40, 42, 43, 46, 47, 49, 51, 53, 54, 55, 56, 58, 59, 60, 61, 65, 68, 69, 70, 71, 74, 75–86, 87, 89, 96, 97, 98, 99, 100, 103, 105, 113, 114, 115, 116
  Conjectural Beginning of Human History 22, 70, 114
  Critique of Judgment 1, 3, 18, 21, 54, 55, 81, 84, 103
  Idea for a Universal History with Cosmopolitan Intent 22
  Religion Within the Bounds of Reason Alone 75
  "What is Enlightenment?" 103
Kerry, Stanley S. 61, 126
Kim, Kwang-Myung 102, 131
Koch, Franz 48–49, 86, 122
Kommerell, Max 39, 40–41, 59, 123
Kontje, Todd 107–108, 131
Koopmann, Helmut 61, 118
Korff, Hermann A. 39, 41–42, 122
Kühnemann, Eugen 26–27, 75, 121

Langer, Susanne K. 67–68, 124
Latzel, Sigbert 80–81, 126
Laube, Heinrich 15, 120
Leibniz, Gottfried W. von 24, 25, 32, 40, 85, 100

Leroux, Robert 39, 55–56, 108, 118, 123
Lessing, Gotthold E. 17, 23, 54, 66, 74
Lohner, Edgar 68, 127
Longinus 54
Lovejoy, Arthur A. 39, 51–53, 111, 122, 123
Lukács, Georg 58, 80, 87–88, 89, 91, 94, 95, 108, 124
Lutz, Hans 46, 47–48, 63, 107, 118, 123

Mackensen, Friedrich A. 8, 9
Mainland, William F. 108, 118
Man, Paul de 83–84, 131
Mann, Thomas 5, 126
Manso, Johann K. F. 8, 9
Marcuse, Herbert 89, 90–91, 92, 93, 107, 114, 125
Marx, Karl 15, 90, 93, 97, 98, 99, 106, 107,
Marx, Wolfgang 112, 131
Marxism, Marxist 34, 56, 58, 80, 84, 86–94, 96, 114
Mehring, Franz 34–35
Meier, Albert 115, 131
Meiners, Christoph 111
Mendelssohn, Moses 53, 54, 61, 74, 104, 111
Meng, Heinrich 50–51, 123
Menzel, Wolfgang 14, 119
Mettler, Heinrich 83, 129
Meyer, Herman 103–104, 126
Meyer, Theodor M. 49–50, 123
Miller, Ronald D. 78, 126
Moritz, Karl P. 32, 49, 51
Muehleck-Müller, Cathleen 103, 131
Mugdan, Bertha 33, 121
Müller, Hermann F. 48, 120, 122
Müller, Joachim 86, 126

National Socialism 39, 42
Neo-Kantianism 20, 23, 26, 27, 32, 33, 37
Neo-Platonism 21, 32, 49, 65, 85, 88
Nicolai, Friedrich 9, 119
Nietzsche, Friedrich 23, 42, 68
Nisbet, Hugh B. 108, 119
Novalis (Friedrich von Hardenberg) 96

Oellers, Norbert 7, 128

Pater, Walter 36
Pascal, Roy 91, 127
Pfeifer, Eleonora 89, 129
Pfotenhauer, Helmut 103, 124
Plato 56, 67, 85
Platonism 21, 36, 48, 52, 53, 57, 85, 86, 88
Plotinus 48, 49, 53, 67, 85
Popitz, Heinrich 107, 124
Pott, Hans-Georg 84, 85, 130
Pugh, David 85–86, 132

Quintilian 104

Read, Herbert 56–57, 124
Reeves, Nigel 91, 102, 129
Redfield, Marc 83–84, 132
Rehm, Walter 50, 115, 123
Reiner, Hans 75, 124
Reiss, Hans 95, 125
Richter, Johann P.(Jean Paul) 11, 119
Rippere, Victoria 106, 130
Robinson, Henry C. 35
Robertson, James G. 37–38, 121
Rohrmoser, Günter 80, 126
Rosalewski, Willy 33, 122
Rousseau, Jean-Jacques 45, 47, 48, 52, 111
Ruge, Arnold 15, 120
Ruppelt, Georg 42
Ruskin, John 36

Saintsbury, George 36, 121
Sartre, Jean-Paul 68, 78
Sautermeister, Gerd 113, 128
Savile, Anthony 66, 131
Sayce, Olive 112, 127
Schaper, Eva 80–82, 127, 130
Scheler, Max 80
Schelling, Friedrich W. J. von 12, 22, 34, 36, 76, 84
Scherer, Wilhelm 31
Schiller, Friedrich
   "Das Ideal und das Leben" 44
   "Der Spaziergang" 70
   Die Braut von Messina 105
   "Die Götter Griechenlands" 50
   "Die Künstler" 18
   Die Räuber 1

Die Schaubühne als eine moralische Anstalt betrachtet 96
Die Verschwörung des Fiesco zu Genua 1
Don Carlos 1, 44
Geschichte des Abfalls der Niederlande 1
Kabale und Liebe 1
Kallias letters xi, 2, 18, 22, 26, 28, 32, 37, 39, 41, 44, 51, 55, 60, 61, 62, 70, 71, 80, 81, 82
Philosophie der Physiologie 62
Schein 4, 17, 35, 36, 37, 67–68, 73, 90, 94, 95, 96, 100, 106, 116
schöne Seele 2, 3, 28, 29, 49, 59, 69
Spieltrieb 4, 16, 25, 36, 45, 52, 66, 97, 107
Stofftrieb 9, 40, 49, 53, 62, 85, 94, 97, 100
sublime 2, 3, 28, 29, 50, 51, 54, 59, 62, 66, 70–75, 82, 84
Theosophie des Julius 40, 43
Über Anmut und Würde 2, 3, 21, 23, 27, 32, 33, 34, 42, 44, 49, 51, 53, 54, 56, 59, 60, 71, 75, 76, 78, 84, 86
Über das Erhabene xi, 4, 17, 21, 22, 29, 32, 44, 61, 65, 70, 72, 73, 86, 98, 108
Über das Pathetische 3, 23
"Über den Gebrauch des Chors in der Tragödie" 105, 108
Über den Grund des Vergnügens an tragischen Gegenständen 3
Über den Zusammenhang der tierischen Natur des Menschen mit seiner geistigen 24
Über die tragische Kunst 3
Über naive und sentimentalische Dichtung 3, 5, 6, 8, 9, 11, 16, 18, 22, 23, 26, 27, 29–31, 33, 35, 36, 39, 45, 50, 52, 55, 61, 65, 72, 73, 78, 89, 91, 92, 98, 108–115, 116
Von notwendigen Grenzen beim Gebrauch schöner Formen 104
Wallenstein 44, 61, 89
Schings, Hans-Jürgen 74, 130
Schlegel, August W. 10, 11, 119
Schlegel, Friedrich 9, 52, 110, 111, 121
Schmeer, Hans 49, 122

Schopenhauer, Arthur 23, 30
Schütz, Christian G. 8, 124
Schütz, Oskar 67
Seidel, Siegfried 86, 89, 109, 126
Shaftesbury, see Anthony Ashley Cooper, Lord
Shakespeare, William 11, 18
Sharpe, Lesley 66, 132
Sime, James 36, 120
Smith, Adam 91
Sommer, Robert 24–25, 28, 33, 48, 49, 102, 121
Spencer, Herbert 36, 52, 57
Spranger, Eduard 43–44, 62, 124
Stahl, Ernst L. 54–55, 123, 124
Strube, Werner 69, 129
Sulzer, Johann G. 111
Szondi, Peter 113, 129

Thomas, Calvin 37, 121
Tomaschek, Karl 22–23, 25, 28, 56, 120
tragedy, Schiller's theory of xi, 3, 54, 73–74, 78, 105
Träger, Claus 89–90, 109, 126
Trieb, Triebe 23, 84, 91, 102
Tschierske, Ulrich 102, 131

Überweg, Friedrich 23, 120
Ueding, Gerd 104, 128

Vergil 114
Viëtor, Karl 54, 123
Vorländer, Karl 27–28, 75, 121
Vulpius, Wolfgang xii

Walzel, Oskar 32–33, 48, 53, 60, 77, 85, 118
Watanabe-O'Kelly 108, 119
Wellek, René 53, 109, 125
Wells, George A. 112, 127
Wersig, Peter xii
Wessell, Leonard P. 69–70, 111, 128, 130
Wieland, Christoph M. 49
Wienbarg, Ludolf 14–15, 119
Wiese, Benno von 59–60, 63, 95, 111, 118, 126, 127
Wilkinson, Elizabeth M. 63–65, 67, 68, 71, 72, 83, 86, 97, 101, 104, 107, 118, 125, 126, 127, 128

Willoughby, Leonard A. 63–65, 71, 72,
    83, 86, 94, 97, 101, 107, 118, 124
Wilm, Emil C. 37, 121
Winckelmann, Johann J. 50, 77, 115
Windelband, Wilhelm 33, 121
Witte, William 59, 85, 95, 124, 126